BLACK AMERICA, INC.

A TRILLION DOLLAR NATION

By A.R. Morton

"I'd rather you hate me and pay me, than to like me and fight me."

- A.R. Morton

Table of Contents

Dedication

I dedicate this book to my beautiful wife Averia and my two amazing daughters Aniyah & Mai. The biggest and most significant reason behind me writing this book was to be able to leave some knowledge with my family that they can use and pass on for generations to come. My wife and my children are my number one motivators in everything that I do. The work that I do to help people comes from the things my wife and children do for me. As a husband and father, I believe it is my duty to guide, protect and provide for my family to the best of my ability at all times. This book is just one of the many examples of what I have been able to accomplish with the tremendous support I get from the three of you. I am grateful for this amazing family we have created. I love you all. Thank you for everything.

Trillion Dollar Nation

Hotep everyone. If you have done any research on the social, political and economic status of the black community, it's plausible you have come across the fact that Black Americans spend over one trillion dollars ($1,100,000,000,000) a year in the US retail market. These projections are expected to rise to 1.3 trillion by the year 2017. Because of this you may have asked *"Why are most Black Americans suffering financially?"* and that is a legitimate question to ask.

The answer is simple; most Black Americans lack the basic financial literacy that is necessary for the accumulation and growth of intergenerational wealth. Ninety-eight percent (98%) of their income is spent with businesses and services established by other ethnic groups and races outside of their communities.

Think about everything you pay a bill on, who owns that service provider? Reflect on the brands you buy the most, who owns it? The stores you shop? What percentage of these things are black owned? People have become so used to being consumers that they don't even care who they buy from and that is keeping them in a perpetual state of financial dependency which transcends into other aspects of society.

To bring it home for me, I imagined the Black American population as one nation and looked at the behavior of every other group in the same lens. The Black American Nation pays every other nation for their wants and needs and produces nothing for themselves. Ironically, if the Black American Nation were to stop relying on these other nations for their goods and services, those nations would suffer an exponential loss in their overall development because eighty-seven percent (87%) of their marketplaces get their funding from ninety-eight percent (98%) of the Black Nation's economy.

Even though Black Americans represent some of the poorest demographics in this country we still somehow find the funds to give to these Big Business corporations to buy new clothes, shoes, hair, electronics, food, entertainment, alcohol, medicine, etc. Black Americans spend nine times more than any other group in this country even though we don't presently own or run any industries. The result of this behavior is the lack of self-sufficiency and practice of group economics within the black community.

If you travel to the Asian communities in your city, most of the businesses there will be run by Asians. This goes for the Jewish, Italian, and Middle Eastern communities as well. Fifty percent (50%) of the entire Asian population in the United States is self-employed, meaning they don't rely on external forces to secure wealth for them and theirs. I bring these examples up to show that it is possible for the black community to become more self-sustaining.

It is a little-known fact that the Black American dollar is one of the most powerful and sought after economic tools prized by industries relying heavily on the consumerism of the Black American populous. However, it is common knowledge that companies like the Nielsen Company and other institutions dedicate significant time and resources to the research and study of the spending habits of Black Americans. The collected data is then stored and distributed to individuals and businesses aiming to effectively market their goods and services to the black consumer.

If you equally divide the yearly expenses of every Black American, you would end up with a little over twenty-two thousand dollars ($22,000) each person. This figure is inclusive of every man, woman, and child.

Based on that math alone it is feasible that with proper financial acumen, black communities can greatly reduce the problems plaguing them in Corporate America and lower income environments. Although there are those who believe white supremacy and its components are the deciding factor in how blacks will fair in this country; I would caution that regardless of any validity to these claims, Black Americans still owe it to themselves and those they care about to find a solution.

We could mention the bombing of Black Wall Street in Tulsa, Oklahoma or we could speak about the heinous acts of violence and abuse from whites towards blacks. We can even talk about the way individual institutions locked black people out of opportunities so that they could cater to the white population, and all of that would be valid. However, what is equally as valid is what we do not discuss which is how most Black Americans have been complacent in their circumstance and how all of this can be changed with financial discipline and proper execution.

The primary goal should be for Black Americans to begin living better and owning more.

To do this black people must first come together on a social, economic, and political basis. It is crucial for the prosperity and sustainability of black communities throughout the country that its residents are at the forefront of their empowerment.

A key factor here is the level of concern Black Americans have with Black American problems in the name of proactivity. Many black people in the United States are working to change the condition of their communities every day, but the numbers are still despairingly small. Because an even larger number of Black Americans are looking for external bodies to come in and change their condition in this country, the level of action to change it themselves decreases.

I want to make this very clear; this book is not an indictment of black citizens in America to shame them in any way. Though there are some troubling truths about the current state of black communities in America, this book is meant to educate and empower, not to belittle or berate. In the twenty-first century, Black Americans have the power, the access to knowledge and resources available to better themselves as a nation. We cannot and should not let the perils of the past dictate what is possible in the here and now. In fact, we should look at the past achievements that we've accomplished in these same points of time and use them as a driving force of our empowerment.

The independent research I've done for the past two years has led me down a rabbit hole of Black American economic possibility. So much so that I had to start writing them down, often in the forms of tweets. The Black American consumption rates in the US market captivated me, especially as a small business owner.

While researching the economics of Black America, I realized the impact of my own spending habits and began to see what I could do to accumulate more wealth for my household. Planning, budgeting, saving and investing practices put my family in a better economic state. Something that will be detailed further in this book is the need to cut back on the consumption of liabilities in the form of non-essential goods and services while building wealth. Seeing how these things helped me and my personal wealth, I thought it would be a crime if I kept these lessons to myself and not share them with others so they could also accumulate some for themselves. I didn't expect the reactions I received.

Now, I won't say that every Black American that I shared this information with were resistant to changing their money management. Some people were open to the ideas and even started implementing them in their personal lives. Unfortunately, the overwhelming majority were not receptive to the information. This reception led me to do more research to find the reason behind this negative mindset and behavior. What I found was a lack of production in the black community which promoted a lifestyle of which I call a "consumption of material happiness" that explained these reactions.

It is thought to be easier to "look" rich than to be rich. It is much simpler to buy an expensive house or car that you may not be able to afford than it is to have money saved and invested so that it accumulates over the short and long term. I underestimated the sheer resilience of Black American consumerism despite the statistics because I hadn't yet seen it be challenged or advised against before I began my research.

Despite these methods being able to help get people out of bad debt and live wealthier lives, I discovered the reluctance to participate was exacerbated by the lifestyles being marketed to them. Clothing and apparel are widely associated with social status regarding the appearance of prosperity within Black America. A person wearing the trendiest or most expensive garments are usually trying to convey that they live a prosperous lifestyle that allows them to afford these items, even though that may not be accurate. Living beyond ones means or "keeping up with the Joneses" has hurt the Black American economy for generations, and despite the backlash, this cannot be ignored. Poor people only see the lives of the rich from the outside looking in so it is easier for them to misconstrue what it means to be wealthy.

In their book *"The Millionaire Next Door: The Surprising Secrets of America's Wealthy"* authors Thomas J. Stanley and William D. Danko explained how most millionaires live well below their means to build wealth. ***"...Nearly three times as many households with investments of $1,000,000 or more living in homes valued at $300,000 or less than there are living in homes valued at $1,000,000 or more."***. This behavior transcends into all other facets of consumption which keep bad expenses low and wealth accumulation high. On the road to wealth accumulation, it is critical that people focus their funds on saving and investing more than splurging on material goods.

What the top dogs in the finance industry don't want the public to know is that economics is not as complicated as one would have you believe. Simply put, economics is a formula that outlines the behaviors of buyers and sellers, consumers and producers. By observing these behaviors, you can create business and institutional models and apply them to maximize profitability and productivity. Economics isn't just about dollars and cents, in fact, you can still have a thriving economy without representative paper currency at all. Whether it be barter and trade or a society built on contributism where each person in any given community contributes something they are truly passionate about for the greater good of them all, or traditional exchange, economics can come in many forms.

I am here to tell you that without financial discipline and power, black people will always be in the position they're in as a collective. Contrary to popular belief, marching and protesting do next to nothing when it comes to seeking change, especially with no backing capital. It appears to be working because people are surrounded by other individuals who are just as emotional, yelling for and demanding something that seems right.

"Martin Luther King and the Civil Rights Movement did it so it MUST be effective, right?" Wrong. If you find yourself fighting for the same things your ancestors did, in the same fashion they did it in, then it's safe to say that it was an overall failed mission. I'm not calling MLK and those who came before me failures. Martin (as well as other leaders) spoke on group economics in the black community. I truthfully don't intend to disrespect anyone; I'm just pointing out a major flaw in the psyche of many young Black Americans that needs redirection before it's too late and honestly, it's been too late for generations.

When it came to fighting for rights, Black Americans believed that inclusion in the white society meant success. That instead of buying, owning and patronizing our coffee shops and diners, we'd much rather march and protest to be able to patronize a white owned one. We demanded white people to "accept" us into their fold and now in 2016; young Black Americans are upset at how whites call the shots inside of the fold and how those shots aren't usually in their best interests.

But why would they be, because it's the "right" thing to do? It's a no for me. That simply is not how this society operates and even if you were going to change that, you would still have to be a master of your society before doing so. I'm not mad white people in white owned institutions look out for other white people first and foremost because I'm most certainly going to do the same in my institutions in their respective condition. Obviously, I am not promoting discriminating against individuals because of their skin color; I am simply promoting job creation in the black community by Black Americans. Call it "white privilege" or whatever you'd prefer, the fact remains, nobody owes you anything just because you believe you deserve it. People complain about white privilege largely because they have nothing they can call their own. If Black Americans had their institutions and businesses, they could serve their people in the same way.

Looking at how much the other nations have accomplished based on the economic truth; it would only make sense that if the Black American Nation kept their funds and then used it for the development of themselves, they would be able to achieve and even surpass the accomplishments of the other nations they previously supported.

One trillion dollars is a large sum of wealth that if used correctly would be the foundation of what all Black Americans in their subconscious want which is total and complete freedom. Just to illustrate that this isn't a fantasy that I am conjuring up from the depths of my imagination, I am going to explain what black people can do with their yearly expenses and what others have been doing with it for centuries.

The first thing Black Americans must do is solidify the bare essentials of a nation: Food, Education, Housing and Clothing. Black Americans must create and organize Boards of Directors for each of these industries and others described in this book to make sure the policies, practices, and laws are upheld and used at all times. That every entity involved is under protection and safe from bad business practices and illegal activity. Having an administrative team in every industry secures the future of the businesses, institutions, and entities that work inside of them. When building a society, it is imperative to make rules that are in the best interest of the population and then have said population follow them to the best of their ability.

Section 1: Food

Black Americans must grow and make their food. Before I detail why this is an important task for the economy of the Black American, I would be doing a major disservice if I didn't speak on the health aspects of eating. The state of health in Black America is in dire straits. As of 2014, over thirty-six percent (36.7%) of Black American men are obese, almost fifty-seven percent (56.9%) for Black American women. Over forty percent (40.9%) of Black American men suffer from Hypertension and almost forty-five percent (44.8%) for Black American women.

Per the American Cancer Association, about two hundred thousand (189,910) new cancer cases were expected to be diagnosed among blacks in 2016. The most commonly diagnosed cancers among men are prostate (31% of all cancers), lung (15%), and colon and rectum (9%). Among black women, the most common cancers are breast (32%

of all cancers), lung (11%), and colon and rectum (9%). African Americans have the highest death rate and shortest survival of any racial and ethnic group in the US for most cancers.

A big reason why so many Black Americans suffer so much with their health is due to the high consumption of some of the unhealthiest foods in this country, full of addictive properties like refined sugar, salts and saturated fats along with a myriad of preservatives and toxic chemicals that affect their genetics and overall health.

If the Black American population plans on moving forward, their physical and mental health should be at the forefront of their minds. It may seem unimportant due to societal indoctrination, but if you do not have your health, you do not have anything. How can you expect you make progress if you're slowly poisoning yourself?

No intelligent military strategist would use sick and unhealthy soldiers in battle, and if this behavior continues it will surely be the end for our people. This is not an exaggeration, and we must take care of this problem as soon as possible. Later in this book, I am going to show you viable options that can be applied.

With the one trillion Black American dollars, we can buy land in the rural and urban areas in any given city or state. If Black Americans use just one percent (1%) of their yearly expenses of ten billion dollars ($10,000,000,000), we could buy an estimate of 3,311,258.3 acres of land or 5,173 square miles. I also want to point out that The United States of America is only 5,057 square miles, coast to coast.

When Black Americans focus their funds on purchasing a variety of rural farmlands as well as inner city lots, they will have the land necessary to grow their food and access to fresh local produce that is void of dangerous, unnatural pesticides and GMOs (Genetically Modified Organisms) with a much shorter farm-to-table timeframe.

This newly purchased land creates jobs for farmhands, gardeners, packers, harvesters and others that are needed to maintain and cultivate the ground every season out of the year. Independent farming would open jobs for hundreds of thousands, if not millions of people because of how large the Black American population is and how much money we spend on food annually in markets. This initiative could also provide homes because the farmhands will have the opportunity to live on the land they are tilling, creating more communities and civil togetherness within the farming industry.

Channeling our funds into the growth of the Black American food industry will open the doors to a national consumer base and the ability to cater to all people. Just as every ethnic group in this country buys produce from Whole Foods and Trader Joe's, they will also patronize the black owned markets and chains out of pure national popularity once Black Americans start shopping with them. Black owned food markets will retail local and national black owned food brands creating a productive cycle of good business.

Creating and patronizing local black owned food markets is paramount. Despite having dozens of local farms, community gardens, and small market infused sections of restaurants, the number of black owned grocery stores is extremely low in America. Building food markets that cater to the dietary and nutritional needs of the community will play a significant role in developing a healthier society.

While I was researching Black American owned grocery stores, I came across the story of Michele and Erich March. Michele Speaks-March and Erich March are founders of the black owned grocery store Apples & Oranges Fresh Market located in Baltimore, Maryland. The March's strived to provide healthier foods options for the surrounding communities to choose from within their store. They offered classes to educate shoppers on the importance of healthy eating. The market didn't supply fried foods, sodas or tobacco products because they believed it wasn't in the best interest of the shoppers to consume those items.

Even though this business sounds lovely on paper, the grocery store had to close its doors just two years after opening, mainly due to lack of financial support in their community. Residents just did not shop at the grocer, saying the products were too expensive. However, one of the bigger reasons was because the grocer didn't supply the highly processed foods they like consuming. If Apples & Oranges weren't going to sell those items, why shop there?

While the March's wanted to provide high quality produce and healthier food alternatives, the residents wanted the microwavable instant meals and fried foods. Despite the push back the March's stood firm on their principles and soon paid the ultimate price after only two years of operation. This type of consumer behavior must change if Black Americans want to prosper as a people.

We shouldn't look at the story of Apples & Oranges and be discouraged; it should show us where we are going wrong and inspire us to make a change. In fact, I propose the communities of Baltimore pool their resources together and contribute to the re-opening of Apples & Oranges Fresh Market. We need more grocers like Apples & Oranges in our communities because as previously stated our eating habits has landed us in a troubling state of perpetual unhealthiness as a people.

This story serves a deeper purpose when we peel back the layers of the Black American diet. For the most part, Black Americans consume cuisine called "Soul Food." Dishes that are predominantly made up of high amounts of unhealthy ingredients like saturated fats refined salts, sugars, and meats. Even though vegetables play a role in the meals, they're usually covered or cooked with those same unhealthy ingredients ultimately neutralizing whatever nutritional value they may have had.

This type of dining has been a part of the Black American culture dating back to slavery, which some people argue it got its roots. The slave master would leave the black slaves the “scraps” and with ingenuity the slaves transformed them into dishes of their own. Others argue that slaves had their own gardens, ate whole grains, fruits, and vegetables and even hunted food. I'm willing to believe that it was a mixture of both and slaves made do with what they had.

Nevertheless, this diet has been passed down for generations, which means Black Americans associate these meals with their history and culture making it difficult to detach themselves from it. Food is a very social aspect of Black American life. Family gatherings, live events, barbeques and holidays of all kinds are centered around food in the black community.

These meals are predominantly made with love and the desire to nourish themselves and others with what they know to be good food. There's an emotional attachment families have with the foods they eat together, and it should be encouraged for more families to participate in this behavior. Family dinners are vital.

"Entertaining is also very important in the African-American community. Annual events such as family reunions, cultural festivals and alumni gatherings connect Blacks in a unique way that focuses on fellowship and is cross-generational. African American households spend more on basic food ingredients and beverages than non-Hispanic Whites, and also value the food preparation process more."

- Nielsen Company, 2015

The average black family just doesn't know the role food plays in their health, on a real nutritional level. For the most part, parents are cooking what was cooked for them, never actually seeking alternatives or different recipes. These recipes are what they know and in the vein of tradition are practiced on a regular basis.

In the same way, the recipes for these meals have been passed down, so have the ailments and diseases that come along with them. Dietary and lifestyle (or preventable) diseases are in abundance in the black community and unfortunately are overlooked in the same vein of tradition. It is often justified with the sentiment *"it runs in my family."* and even accepted as an inevitability in a lot of cases.

While there is some credence to genetic and hereditary conditions, diseases like diabetes, high blood pressure, and cancer are preventable when one chooses to live a healthier lifestyle. As time goes on, more and more Black Americans are understanding this and are making better health decisions overall.

Per the Nielsen Company, seventy-nine percent (79%) of African American women believe pursuing good health is important. When you combine that statistic with the statistic from the Bureau of Labor Statistics (BLS) that reports eighty-five percent (85%) of American women do the housework including meal preparation and cooking, we can conclude that the healthier the women are, the healthier their families will be.

Black American wives and mothers are becoming increasingly interested in healthier lifestyle options which show through the foods they prepare and the activities they engage. When the cooks of the home start preparing healthier meals, everyone who eats it will become healthier.

Investing between five hundred thousand and one million dollars ($500,000-$1,000,000) in each grocery store will allow us to build, operate and provide food for the communities which save shoppers in transportation and food costs. The food intiative also provides shelf space for local food and lifestyle businesses alike to retail their goods. This relationship between grocery stores and manufacturers is a fundamental principle in local business.

Local grocery stores can be economic hubs in their area. The local grocers have the ability to showcase different small businesses in their stores which maximize the exposure and patronage of their goods. Community gardens and urban farms are now able to make a profit by selling their harvest yields to the grocery stores in their area. Local bakers and cooks can sell their foods in the store. Local health & beauty aid businesses can retail their products on the store's shelves. Small kitchenware, toiletry, and cleaner manufacturers can now not only supply shoppers with their goods, but they can also be used in the store itself.

When these brands do well, they become more valuable in the markets, and when the markets do well, they promote more patronage to the brands they shelve. Our grocery stores can take notes from Apples & Oranges and provide classes and workshops for people to learn about nutrition, alternative meals and how to prepare them. The owners and representatives of the local brands and farms can come to the stores and provide "demos" of their goods where shoppers can sample and learn more about them. These types of interactions between producers and consumers are what makes a household name.

This initiative encourages aspiring young black restaurateurs to open up shop and start their businesses. Restaurant owners, like the market owners, will be supplied with the foods from the black owned farms throughout the nation assuring the highest quality of nutrition and health possible for those that eat there. Restaurateurs even have the possibility of supplying their own produce. Imagine seeing restaurants in your city or town with food gardens on the roof or in the backyard. Having your food prepared with the freshest ingredients possible will help do away with the stigmas against the cleanliness of restaurants and the quality of their foods. Growing produce also helps cut one of the biggest costs for restaurant owners, food inventory. Up to forty percent (40%) of restaurants' expenses are made of up the cost of food.

A prime example of this would be The Rooftop Farm of the eco-friendly and sustainable restaurant Uncommon Ground in Chicago, Illinois. The 654-square foot certified organic farm (which also carries several beehives) yields 800 pounds of produce a growing season, not enough to supply the restaurant's needs but enough to cut costs on food production and increased the quality of foods. The restaurant also offers weekly tours for the public and summer internships for aspiring urban farmers. Sustainable restaurants like these are the best option for public dining in the black community and it is becoming increasingly possible for Black Americans to participate and profit from it.

According to the National Restaurant Association, restaurant industry sales are expected to reach seven hundred and eighty-three billion dollars ($783,000,000,000) in 2016, a one hundred-billion-dollar increase from 2014's projection. These figures let us know that starting and running restaurants in the black community proves to be a very lucrative field to participate in economically.

Investing between five hundred thousand and one million dollars ($500,000-$1,000,000) will cover the costs of building a fully functional restaurant with all the amenities that come with it. As we saw with Uncommon Ground, our restaurants have the ability to grow their produce and offer plant based dishes on their menus. Our restaurants can also participate in providing catering services for social and formal events of all kinds being planned throughout the city.

Our restaurants will be able to offer delivery services just like the major food retailers do, but with higher quality meals. Having nutritional-based restaurants in the black community will provide an alternative to the unhealthier options like Fast Food restaurants. Our restaurants should be businesses that promote healthy living along with delicious foods, where people can go to get a decent meal in a family oriented environment.

Restaurants don't have to be the rundown establishments that we may see in our areas today. Every restaurateur deserves the opportunity to build a business that prides itself on serving the very best foods available, along with the very best service from the very best staff. Individuals, couples, and families alike can sit and enjoy their meals all while having a high quality restaurant experience.

As we will learn further into this book, honing and using our skills to grow our food will be the single most independent and revolutionary thing we can do as individuals. When you have the control over your food supply, you have the ability always to feed yourself and others which is essential to a fruitful nation.

Not only that, "putting food on the table" has long been one of the main reasons people seek employment and generate income. When you grow your food, feeding your family won't be the most significant factor when it comes to your pursuit of happiness. This allows people to choose career paths that are more conducive to their lifestyle rather than taking any job to sustain themselves.

This initiative works its way into the Education section as well. Having agricultural programs embedded in the curriculum of all schools at every grade level is imperative. Teaching the generations to come how to grow their foods and to use nature as their primary source for all things, including utility and medicine.

Circling back to health, Black Americans can use the resources grown from the black owned farms to help heal, and in a lot of cases cure what is ailing them. Growing and maintaining the herbs and roots that provide proven medicinal properties coupled with the fruits, vegetables, nuts, grains, legumes, spices, and seeds that provide the same, as well as an active lifestyle will ensure guaranteed good health and long life for all those who participate.

Herbs and roots like Ginkgo Biloba, St. John's Wort, Kava Kava, Goldenseal, Ginger, Turmeric, Chamomile, Catnip, Aloe, Echinacea, Anise, Cloves, Burdock, Calendula, Garlic, Cinnamon, Dandelion, Coriander, Basil, Thyme, Rosemary, Willow Bark, Elderberry, Spirulina, Moringa, Marjoram and hundreds more all have incredible healing powers that we should all take advantage of. Remaining within the one percent (1%) of the Black American annual budget, we can open up several Holistic Health Centers across the country. Having established Holistic Health Centers gives our people an alternative to the norms of Western Modern Medicine where they are more likely to prescribe a patient drugs or suggest surgery before anything that pertains to nature and her healing powers.

Given the statistics stated above coupled with the report from the WHO (World Health

Organization) that says the global pharmaceutical market is projected to see a one hundred billion dollar increase by 2019, we can conclude that Black Americans being perpetually sick is big business for those who stand to make a profit. The average Western doctor, medical or otherwise keeps these giants in business by prescribing you their products, drugs.

Because the Black American population makes up eighty-seven percent (87%) of the overall US market and are the most affected by health problems it shows just how important it is to undo the cycle of bad lifestyle choices and diets even on an economical level. A theme that will be consistent throughout this book is just how much money the Black American saves by being overall self-sufficient. In this case, the less money you have to spend on medical expenses and prescription drugs, the more money you have to your name.

Just think about how much money you would save if you didn't have to pay for the medications you're currently taking and replacing them with natural resources that are biologically created to reproduce for long term use.

Another crucial issue is the American water supply. As we've seen in recent times, the water supply of many cities across this country is contaminated with poisons like lead, mercury, and fluoride, leaving the people who drink, cook and bathe in it with weaker immune systems, bones, and sometimes even losing their lives. Water is essential to our livelihood; we cannot survive without water. Humans are made up of seventy-five percent (75%) water, and if the water supply is contaminated, then the people are left without their life's essence.

The solution is drilling water wells and creating facilities that will be able to run, test, filter, purify and supply the communities with a viable water source. Being able to use the technology available to clean the current water systems is also a priority. Black Americans will also have independent water wells throughout the communities as an option for residents accompanied with faucet filters for all homes. Once we gain control of our food and water supply, the current state of health of the Black American population would almost reverse completely because diet and water were the main factors in how they became sick in the first place.

Section 2: Education

Knowledge is power and ignorance is weakness. For far too much time the Black American education system failed its students, teachers, and parents. Areas with a high concentration of black students are littered with underperforming schools; leading examples are cities like Detroit, Chicago, and the New York City boroughs. The children that attend these schools are not intellectually inferior by nature, but when they are forced to learn in environments that are not conducive to gaining and retaining knowledge they will almost always fall short.

To get to the solution, we must fully understand the problem with the education of our people, mainly our youth. In a report from the U.S Department of Education experts revealed ***"A higher percentage of Black and Hispanic students attended high-poverty schools (as determined by the percentage of students in school eligible for the***

free and reduced-lunch program) than did students of other racial/ethnic groups, while a lower percentage of Asian/Pacific Islander and White students attended high-poverty schools."

Black American boys are especially affected by these environments. According to PBS just a little over half of all Black American children (54%) graduate from high school. Black male students are two and a half times more likely to be suspended than white students. Black American males only make up five and a half percent (5.5%) of all college students according to the Congressional Black Caucus Foundation. Our children need our help, and they need it fast.

It is a fact that children being raised in poverty have the hardest time being able to excel in schools. The living conditions and present environment stresses these children to the point of mental and sometimes physical exhaustion, leaving them discouraged and unwilling to do well academically. Unmotivated children in an era where it is increasingly easy to be distracted by technology, media, and inappropriate behavior is a recipe for disaster for the future of our people. Our children are stifled in their mental development before they can have a fighting chance in the classroom because of their surroundings.

Parents' education plays a major role in a child's development as well. According to the same U.S Department of Education report, ***"Research has shown a link between parental education levels and child outcomes such as educational experience, attainment, and academic achievement."***, Simply put, smart parents make for smart children, and the more parents participate in their child(ren)'s education, the more those children excel in school.

Children need parents who value gaining knowledge for themselves. Parents should always be actively educating themselves, so they are better equipped to teach and pass on knowledge to their children which strengthens their relationship when it comes to scholarship. This creates and perpetuates a higher standard of learning which will end in an increase of intelligent black children. Learning together as a family makes it much easier to excel in school because the child's education is being proactively reinforced in the home.

The state of schools in Black America is suffering. Our children are forced to attend some of the worst schools in the country, complete with low expectations for them to attain a thorough education from parents and faculty. Our communities are overrun with public schools that fail to meet the required standards for an institution that facilitates adequate learning. Outdated books, deceitful curriculum, lack of supplies, dangerous and high risk environments, unsanitary classrooms and bathrooms, unhealthy breakfast and lunch options, unenthused staff and faculty, low wages for said staff and faculty, little to no extracurricular activities and external educational programs, overcrowded classes and severe punishment are issues that run rampant in our public schools across the United States and Black Americans, for the sake of our youth must bring this to a complete stop and reversal.

Just like in the Food section, these problems have solutions within building a solid economic foundation in the black community. If you live in any major city in this country, then there's a huge possibility you have an abandoned school (or few) in your neighborhood. What most people see as the failure of a school that once was, I see as an opportunity to rebuild and reopen a school for the children in that area.

Children are wired by their genetics to want to learn; it's instinctual to acquire knowledge because it allows you and your species to live longer. All a child does from the moment they are pushed out of the womb is learn, and we can take advantage of this by building and facilitating the absolute best conditions for optimal learning. In this initiative, if Black Americans invested ten percent

(10%) of the yearly expense at one hundred billion dollars ($100,000,000,000) they could build new layouts for classrooms, gyms and auditoriums, reconfigure and reconstruct the current curriculum, and change lives. Proper funding offers schools frequent workshops for teachers and aspiring teachers to stay up to date on how to effectively teach the youth specific to that school body.

Reestablishing and introducing programs and internships for students to gain real life experience in their desired fields. Giving frequent workshops for parents and students, showing them how they can work together to make sure their children are as successful as possible while also educating the parent on the curriculum. Incorporating a health and diet breakfast and lunch program (stemming from the institutions mentioned in the Food section) that provides the students with a fresh and well balanced meal twice a day, and provide scholarships to certain corporations, colleges or universities within the black community.

This is just a short list of the things that Black Americans can provide its youth if we properly channel the funding. The construction of the Campus Master Plan for the Jesuit High School in Tampa, Florida is a project that I discovered while reading on the internet one day. The campus includes a two-story, collegiate-style Student Activities Center, a 500-seat Dining Hall, Fine and Performing Arts Center with a 450-seat theater/auditorium, and a new two-story, state-of-the-art Science and Math building. The average cost to build or renovate a school is between thirty and fifty million dollars; the Jesuit model is recorded to cost thirty-five million dollars ($35,000,000).

The Black American population can build and renovate a little over 200 schools a year with just ten percent (10%) of the yearly expenses if properly applied. This initiative is not limited to primary and secondary schooling; Black Americans can create academic institutions on a collegiate and university level as well. Building illustrious campuses that cater to the wants and needs of the college and university communities across the country would make attending school more attractive for young adults who are looking to further their education.

Just like the money we spend, this initiative is about bringing the black academic back to its community so he or she can assist in its development and growth instead of utilizing it elsewhere for other communities. Meaning most of our graduating classes will be working in institutions created in black communities across this country, adding to the value of themselves as well as the institution therein.

Our doctors will be working in black owned hospitals and practices; our lawyers will be working in black owned firms and courts; our scientists will be working in black owned laboratories, etc. All of this will strengthen our academic progression as well as our business and professional presence nationally, and even globally. Just imagine your child growing up going to a black owned primary school then graduating to a black owned secondary school then graduating to a black owned university and then working in or creating a black owned business.

It is no secret that American universities provide top studies that affect millions of lives across the country and the globe. Once we build our facilities, we will be able to conduct experiments that will promote the advancements of our people and others. Instead of waiting for the newest findings, we will be the ones discovering and uncovering new (and old) information and applying it to our daily lives. We will have the capacity to patent new inventions and innovations and share them with the world.

Before I continue, I want to make it very clear that I am not excluding any other group from being able to participate in these initiatives, just that these initiatives specifically are created so Black Americans control and run them, primarily. These initiatives will surely affect more groups than just the black population because of how prevalent the black dollar is to the American economy, but it is very important that Black Americans take the reins of their destiny and steer it in the right direction.

This initiative will be able to give all staff and faculty full benefits and living compensation for all the work they do. The importance of properly funding teachers cannot be understated because too often are teachers left without any resources if they don't pay for it themselves. This initiative will supply the teachers with all the necessary equipment they need to properly teach a class without having to come out of pocket for it.

This initiative will cater to underperforming students to make sure they are learning at the proper levels, decreasing the dropout rates and the need for career long special education. This initiative will however, provide special education programs for the students that need it. All of this is possible with just ten percent (10%) of the Black American annual expense.

Black American intelligence and ingenuity have been at the forefront of American development for generations, and it's time to reclaim and operate in the capacities that we instinctively know we can achieve. We cannot forget or celebrate enough the students that are striving for excellence and achieving amazing goals on their academic career path.

Our youth can achieve extraordinary heights when they have a solid home foundation and proper education. Students like Stephen R. Stafford II, who at the age of eleven enrolled into Morehouse College after being homeschooled by his mother is a perfect example of what our children can do. Stephen graduated with a triple major in Pre-Med, Mathematics and Computer Science, with plans to complete Medical School by 2020.

The Imafidon's, officially the smartest family in the United Kingdom: twins Paula and Peter along with their sisters Anne-Marie, Christina and Samantha are another great example. The Imafidon children have broken a plethora of world records in academia and athletics. Anne-Marie was the youngest person in the United Kingdom to pass the UK A-Level Computing Exam at thirteen. Samantha passed two high school level math and statistics tests when she was just six years old. Twins Peter and Paula achieved the honor of being the youngest students in British history to attend high school at nine years old. Christina was the youngest student in history to be accepted to an undergraduate institution at eleven years old.

I believe we all want our children to achieve goals in the same vein as Stephen and the Imafidon children. I also believe we have the power to make it happen. Black Americans have the ability to make these extraordinary performances a normality in the community. All it takes is for us to build these educational institutions and follow through with the education process in the home.

Homeschooling is an option that more and more parents are considering in today's climate. About two and a half million children are being homeschooled in the United States. Homeschooling allows parents to create curriculums that are specific to their children's needs. Biologically, parents are a child's first and most influential teachers they have, so it makes it easier for them to absorb the information. Children have a deeper connection and trust built around the relationship they have with their parents than their teachers. So, when they are learning at home, they are more confident that the knowledge is vital for their wellbeing.

Homeschooling gives the parent and child full control of what the curriculum entails. As I've mentioned, most public schools don't teach adequate Black/African history or social studies among many other pertinent things like wealth management in their classrooms. While the initiatives stated above help solve these problems, a more immediate solution is teaching Black American children these things in the home.

According to the National Home Education Research Institute (NHERI) ***"The home-educated typically score 15 to 30 percentile points above public-school students on standardized academic achievement tests. (The public-school average is the 50th percentile; scores range from 1 to 99.) A 2015 study found Black homeschool students to be scoring 23 to 42 percentile points above Black public school students."*** Meaning academically, homeschooled children have a higher propensity to score above the national average on achievement tests.

There are many positives to switching or pursuing home education instead of the societal norm of compulsory schools. Homeschooling is what led the young Stephen R. Stafford to college before his twelfth birthday. I advise any parent that's willing and able to homeschool their children to try it out for at least a year and see if there is an improvement in your child's development.

Section 3: Housing

The homelessness problem in the United States is severe. Right now, there are more abandoned homes (14.2 Million) than there are homeless people (3.5 Million, 2.5 of which are children) in this country and there's something incredibly wrong about that. Just like the abandoned schools in the Education section, if Black Americans purchase, renovate, rent out and sell the abandoned homes in our communities we could end American Homelessness as we know it.

Here's the math: The average American home is about 2,400-2,600 square feet. The average cost to renovate a house is approximately between twenty-five and fifty dollars ($25-50) a square foot. If we wanted to restore ten thousand (10,000) homes a year it would cost approximately a little over one billion dollars ($1,300,000,000), less than half of a percent (0.5%) of the yearly Black American expense to do so. As with the Education and the Food section, we can use more capital if need be.

Even though the number of abandoned homes is ridiculously high, we should look at this as an opportunity to revitalize our communities. The current and future generations can customize the landscape of their environment. Ranch homes, row homes, colonial homes, condos and apartment buildings and much more can be built in our community as opposed to the rundown homes and project buildings we may be used to.

In 2014, property developing company Secure Realty, LCC renovated a home in Detroit, Michigan suitably named "The Lorax House" due to the sculpture and mural of the famous Dr. Seuss character on the front lawn. The home was vacant for over ten years and was in danger of collapsing. Now it is a revitalized energy efficient building that offers three one-bedroom studio apartments with other amenities built with local creatives in mind.

The art outside of the newly restored home was done by Michigan residents, allowing local artists to showcase their talents and opportunity to gain exposure. Building and running our realtor and property developing companies is essential to property ownership in the black community.

In fact, there are several black owned real estate companies we can choose from today, the largest being The Peebles Corporation. The Peebles Corporation and others like them can transform communities into places better suited to perpetuate excellence in the services they provide. Combining the proposals of community development from local architects and designers along with the resources that a real estate investment company has to offer, Black Americans can begin to establish and renovate the buildings we commune to, work and live in.

This initiative has the potential to end what we know as the "Ghetto." which is necessary for Black America. The importance of the home should not be understated when it comes to the impact it has on the lives in it. Your home is an extension of how you look at yourself.

People innately want clean streets and beautifully built homes, regardless of race. People in visually appealing and attractive neighborhoods have higher expectations for themselves and others, they have a greater chance of being financially successful, a higher chance of having a broader world view, a higher chance of not committing crimes and even living longer. The ghetto does the opposite for its residents.

The ghetto creates and perpetuates a state of disparity, hopelessness, and fear. The ghetto encourages and promotes bad lifestyle choices which can result in a lifetime in prison or death. The ghetto discourages the residents to strive to be the best they can be. Even though we have a small percentage of people that "make it out the hood", this should not overshadow the majority that don't. In fact, "making it out" as a concept wouldn't even make sense if the environment these people were from weren't ghettos. For instance, you don't hear success stories of people "making it out" of Beverly Hills.

Renovating the low-income areas of America is something that I've always believed was vital for the development of this country. As I got older and realized it was possible, it gave me hope for the future. The Lorax House isn't the only example of structural rejuvenation we can observe. The remodeling of an old abandoned electric power station that was renovated in Philadelphia, Pennsylvania also comes to mind. The building is now a complex that hosts forty apartments, twenty parking spaces, and thirteen bike spaces. This just serves as another example of what is possible when we come together to make a change in our neighborhoods' conditions.

Black American cities and towns don't have to be places that people must fight to grow away from; they can instead grow within them and reverse the environmental conditioning people have been accustomed. Even if you plan on moving from your low-income area, please do understand that doing what you can to help your old neighborhood is just as important. A massive preliminary step would be changing the landscape of the environment, renovating abandoned homes and setting a new standard of the community for the people to uphold. This initiative will help change the mindset that has perpetually discouraged Black Americans who have accepted that they and their families will be doomed to live in poverty for the rest of their lives.

Home is where the heart is. Everything we know and do begins in the home. This initiative enforces the importance of culture cultivation, education and wellbeing in the Black American home. A well-kept home allows the household members to interact and maintain together in a more harmonious fashion. Those behaviors will travel with them when they are in school, work or moving about in the community. Residents will have a higher sense of belonging and connection to where they live which results in a collective effort to keep it clean and presentable.

This initiative like all the others creates jobs for contractors, construction workers, landscapers, plumbers, architects, real estate investors, property managers, electricians, engineers, material manufacturers, etc. When we hire these professionals to do their jobs we supply them with the necessary capital to expand and enlarge their businesses. The more jobs and money the company gets, the more people the company can hire to get the work done. This initiative does its part in reducing unemployment rates drastically in the short and long term which will subsequently reduce the crime rate due to the higher concentration of workers and scholars in any given community.

When people live is neighborhoods that are filled with beautiful art and architecture, all of the homes are structurally sound and have attractive curb appeal, the grass, bushes, and flowers are all manicured and landscaped to perfection, the overall mindset of the residents that live there are to preserve the integrity and beauty of their environment.

This means no littering, loitering, trespassing or crimes against your neighbors. Even the worst neighborhoods you've seen have had a connected public system in place at one point in time. However, due to many factors, these places are now some of the most dangerous places to call home. It doesn't have to be this way, and quite frankly, it shouldn't be.

We now have the solution to problems that have been plaguing us for generations. We can rebuild our communities and put them back into a place of prosperity and happiness. Humans are instinctively social creatures; we thrive off interaction with one another. It is the reason we're breathing today. Our parents came together, in one moment, formed a union and created life, us.

Human progression will always be about coming together for the greater good of the whole.

When our communities are intact we are promoting a behavior that keeps families safe, businesses afloat, crime low with productivity and spirits high. People will be more inclined to invite their neighbors over for combined household activities like dinners and cookouts, indoor and outdoor gaming, entertainment or even trips and vacations, strengthening the bond between residents. Participating in these activities brings the trust back into our neighborhoods.

Communities will be more willing to attend council meetings and become more active in their local politics, even influencing them to create political parties and organizing on behalf of themselves (which we will discuss further in the book). Parents will have more time to be a part of their children's education. There are a lot of things a unified community can get done when they're backed up by capital and it is high time that the

Black American population, a trillion-dollar nation, executes this model.

Now, I fully understand that one hundred percent of the black population will not participate in these initiatives, just like any other group. I am however showing that even with the minority of people who will not participate, the overwhelming majority will outweigh and prevail in the long term. Despite the conditioning of a potentially dangerous environment, people want to live prosperous lives. This initiative's economy relies on the community to keep supplying itself with the necessary resources for advancement and growth.

This is why we see active communities patronize the stores in their neighborhoods before anywhere else. Support all the ethical locally owned stores and shops in your community and you will always have a cyclical stream of revenue to thrive off that ciculates several times before it is spent outside its perimeters.

Black Americans' awareness and concern for the future and current state of gentrification in their communities has been rising over time and the only way to combat that is to purchase the properties in our areas. This type of migration into the black community is due to the economic incentives people receive to move there, the overall lack of black ownership of the real estate that is built there, and low political representation and participation. Black Americans must see what the entities that are gentrifying their community are doing and mimic their behavior to their benefit.

On a macro level, rebuilding and revitalizing an area isn't a bad thing. What makes it wrong is the residents of that community aren't the ones doing the rebuilding. Allowing external contractors, property developers and businesses like it to do this work instead of the community's residents. This gives these businesses the last word on who lives where and how.

Many residents are displaced because they can no longer afford to live due to increased property values. We've read the stories, witnessed it or even dealt with it, but have we ever considered why this happens? What goes into the property value when rebuilding and what causes it to shoot up to such high numbers?

There are several factors come into play when dealing with property values and pricing: location and land; surrounding home and businesses; residents and surrounding neighbors; median incomes; the current market status; convenience and accessibility among other things like taxes and profitability are considered when evaluating or pricing a property. Because of this, it is cost effective for these property developers and people in business to buy up low income properties, renovate and market them at prices that attract individuals with higher income levels.

This of course forces the current or former residents to move from these areas into even smaller concentrated areas, leaving them disproportionately disinvested in once again. This has been happening for decades in this country, and Black Americans have the capital and resources necessary to change this housing dynamic. Black Americans must proactively develop their communities instead of waiting for, expecting or reacting to when other groups do it.

The owners and developers set the value and price of the property, and when the residents take control of the developing, a few things happen. The local economy increases because local businesses are executing the developing. The subsequent rise in employment also comes with an increase of income for residents. The companies can source renewable alternatives to building and developing materials which will help cut the cost of construction. Because the development is eco-friendly and sustainable, this decreases our carbon footprint and makes the homes more affordable.

Sustainable building materials will play a major role in the development of Black America. Being able to utilize materials that can be grown out of the ground will prove most lucrative for a thriving society because the supply has a lower tendency to "run out" or be depleted. Materials like recycled steel, straw bales, solar roofing, earth (dirt), Hempcrete and much more are the present and future of architectural technology. Studying and mastering these techniques will be how Black Americans combat the current state of homelessness and poverty from a structural standpoint.

When you combine all these factors, you will see Black Americans can revitalize their communities without having to sacrifice its current residents while also attracting other people with potentially higher incomes to live and visit. Instead of building homes and structures in low income areas that will ultimately displace the people living there, we will do it in the name of community and prosperity.

This initiative focuses on the empowerment of the people and the places they call home. The mission is to help change the way the people feel about themselves through changing the way their community looks. It has been proven that human life is better off and more productive in environments that build their esteem and character. Black Americans, like anybody else, deserve to live in places like this and it's up to us to make it happen. Poverty and homelessness are illogical concepts, and now more than ever we have the power to stop it.

Section 4:

Clothing & Apparel

Black Americans love to dress. It is no secret that the style of the Black American has been one of the most, if not the most dominant style this country has ever seen. From the way that we talk, walk, sing, dance, act, and yes even the way we dress, the Black American has been at the forefront even if it may have been represented by other groups.

Black people set the trends in the United States, and the companies that make billions from our styles knows this the most. The Nielsen Company reports ***"The power of Black influence is something businesses, and content creators must consider when developing strategic marketing campaigns and programs not only for African-Americans but for the general population, too."***

Black Americans must be able to produce their clothing, not only because it strengthens the economy, keeping the funds within their community, but it also helps stop the inhumane business practices clothing companies use domestically and abroad.

Slave and prison labor, extremely low wages, physical and mental abuse and poor working conditions affect millions of people every year. Thousands of sweatshop workers have perished in the making of our favorite clothes and if we're going to stand up and demand justice from a system that exploits its citizens, we cannot with good conscience support these types of brands at the same time.

Because the Black American spends more money, which in turn means they buy more clothing, Black Americans are funding the same oppressive systems some proclaim they don't condone. Our clothing does not need to be made by underpaid, overworked, abused sweatshop workers.

Our clothing can be ethically sourced locally and abroad without compromising our integrity, dignity and overall humanity for a dollar.

Our clothing can be made in our communities by our friends, families, and neighbors. There are plenty of small black owned clothing brands that could be competing with giants like NIKE, Forever 21, H&M, Ralph Lauren, American Apparel and the like if the Black American population just produced and bought their clothes instead. You must understand that the Black American economy helps tremendously in keeping those great businesses afloat in America.

For a quick example, the ever-popular cognac, Hennessy. Fifty to eighty percent (50-80%) of their US sales comes from the Black American economy. Meaning if blacks were to stop buying Hennessy, the company could go out of business in America. That is a power we must focus in our backyards as soon as possible.

The solution is simple; Black Americans must supply their fabrics and factories to produce their clothing with little to no middle men. It is not enough to buy plain T-shirts from larger companies like Hanes or Gildan and then print designs on them; we must grow our supplies and create our clothing factories.

A good example of this are the two sustainable clothing factories of Brandix Apparel Solutions, Ltd. in India which holds the Eco Factory Attribute, an award given by the UK-based retail manufacturer Marks & Spencer's (M&S) "Plan A" initiative. The factory has reduced their energy and water consumption by thirty percent (30%), recycles and reuses one hundred percent (100%) of their solid waste among other great environmentally friendly initiatives that reduce their overall carbon footprint. The factory cost two and a half million dollars ($2,500,000) to build and renovate.

When we invest three million dollars ($3,000,000) in each factory, we will be able to build and renovate these same type of sustainable manufacturing facilities. The abandoned factories that we may see in our towns and cities can be transformed into vibrant workplaces that provide the necessary goods for people to thrive without having to outsource them from foreign places unethically.

Black Americans manufacturing their clothing allows clothing brands to get their fabrics and fibers directly from the source. Black owned clothing brands will be able to buy plain apparel and customize them to sell to the public. This keeps much of the money we spend on Apparel and Services inside the Black American economy.

Per the BLS, ***"Employment in the apparel manufacturing industry has declined by more than 80 percent (from about 900,000 to 150,000 jobs) over the past two decades."*** Throughout this book, we will see how a nation widely depending on external entities and other countries to produce their goods and services, though at lower retail prices, ultimately destabilizes that dependent society.

So, despite U.S citizens spending over two hundred and twenty billion dollars ($222,535,600,000) on Apparel & Services in 2014, U.S apparel manufacturers only brought in a little under seven billion dollars ($6,784,500.000), just three percent (3%) of what was spent. When scaled for Black America the percentage is closer to zero because Black Americans do not own any clothing manufacturing companies. The Black American Apparel manufacturing industry will be a force to reckon with once established.

This initiative does not exclude the smaller fashion houses and boutiques which make limited, custom handmade garments. The sector of high end fashion in Black American Apparel will show and prove to be a groundbreaking endeavor when they acquire proper funding. Investing between one hundred thousand to two hundred and fifty thousand dollars ($100,000-$250,000) in each fashion house gives designers the necessary capital to purchase all the supplies and materials to produce their clothing.

Instead of only paying top dollar for a custom Donatella Versace piece, Black Americans can spend that amount of money with black fashion designers that produce garments of the same or higher caliber. It has been well documented that Black Americans create and stay on top of the latest trends in fashion and now we will be able to profit from it like never seen before.

Fabric among other supplies is extremely crucial to the development of any clothing industry. While the material is imperative, the sustainability of that fabric is just as, if not more important. The industry isn't just about making money; we also want to ensure we are working with planet earth and not against it. Cotton is more than likely the most known fabric used in textile and clothing production today, but what many do not know is that cotton isn't a very sustainable fiber crop and does some considerable damage to the planet when trying to manufacture it for mass production.

Even though cotton farming only takes up two and a half percent (2.5%) of the world's agricultural land, it takes in sixteen percent (16%) of the world's pesticides and almost seven percent (6.8%) of the world's herbicides. Not only that, cotton requires seven hundred to two thousand gallons of water per pound of fiber. Cotton, depending on whether it's grown organically or not can require from two and a half to three and a half acres per ton of fiber. As we can see, cotton isn't at the top of the list when it comes to sustainable fabrics.

Luckily Mother Nature and all her splendor have given us more eco-friendly fibers we can use to make our clothing. Fibers like tencel, bamboo, polyester, and hemp have all been proven to be environmentally and economically better for manufacturers and consumers alike. These fibers require less land and water to yield sizable crops and unlike cotton, return nutrients back to the soil.

Hemp is one of the most versatile plants on earth and a more durable and renewable fabric for clothing than cotton. Even though growing and selling hemp plants in the United States is presently Federally illegal we can still source the material made from hemp without any worries of law enforcement because it is not in plant form. It is completely legal to buy and sell hemp byproduct in the United States.

If we are going to source any organic materials for manufacturing from foreign nations, I would suggest the continent of Africa to be at the top of that list. Not only is Africa he most bountiful continent on the planet, but these business interactions will also build cultural connections between African Nations and Black Americans. Since the severing of our ancestors from their homelands, the relationship between Africans countries and Black America has suffered over generations.

There is an apparent disconnection between some of these nations, but an unfortunate commonality many of us have is the economic disparities we see every day. One of the best ways for Black Americans to reconnect with their corresponding continental nations is through good business practices, helping one another to rebuild infrastructure in their critical areas of need. The money the countries accumulate from supplying Black America and other nations will be used to revitalize their communities in some of the same ways we see in this book.

It is well known that Africa has been used for her resources since the beginning of time and it still happens to this day. Other nations from other continents reap the benefits of what Africa and Africans have to offer the world while Africa sees the least of these developments. This exploitation will be challenged and reversed with the economic and cultural partnerships we all create and maintain with each other.

I understand and respect that there are plenty of countries and islands that black people in America have their roots. This initiative isn't to belittle or to disregard anyone's ethnic backgrounds, but to add to it. The programming of Western civilization has indoctrinated Black Americans with their education and lifestyles to the point that we don't identify with Africa or any other continent that make up our cultural roots.

While we know many Black Americans (and all human life for that matter) are genetically traced back to Africa and even identify as an "African-American,", they still don't draw cultural connections based on these things.

I also acknowledge that there are ancient human fossils that were found in North and South America, concluding that black people did inhabit the continents way before the Transatlantic Slave Trade. As we can see, it is critical for Black Americans to begin actual interaction with their continents and countries of origin to rediscover their beginnings.

This initiative is not exclusive to any one country as we know Africa is a vast body of land that encompasses the most diverse population of people on Earth. Knowing where you come from is something that other American born citizens with immigrant ancestry do, either through cultural tradition in their households or self-discovery. Knowing where you come from is an essential piece to your progress in moving forward. Not to be used to stay complacent and reminiscent of yesteryear, but to learn, adjust and apply in present times.

Through Fairtrade and ethical business practices we can establish international relationships with African countries that mutually benefit all parties involved. These trade deals help strengthen the African economies, allowing them to continue their development as nations all while strengthening the Black American infrastructure. These business relationships are not beholden to African countries only and can be applied anywhere in the world that will allow it.

When we secure our international sources and resources, we can then market to other nations as well, expanding our national economy through a global market. This initiative will allow us to employ our fashion designers, dress makers, tailors, models, photographers, fashion journalists, etc. and build a fashion industry that competes with New York Fashion Week, Paris and others. The factories we build will employ thousands, even millions of workers in the community again chipping more away at the unemployment rate. I believe that when a nation of people manufactures their wants and needs, they are more appreciative of the process and are overall wealthier.

Overall, people will be less likely to waste their possessions because they know what it took to create it. Also, the quality of the product will have increased because of the centralized sourcing of the raw materials, which prolongs the life of the good. So instead of discarding a shirt after a year of wear, either because you don't value it anymore or it has holes in it, you will be able to wear your locally manufactured clothing longer and stronger.

These are general examples that are applicable in the here and now. When we iron out all the details, placing all the proper people in their respective positions the execution process will be efficient and expedient. Black Americans owe it to themselves to dominate the fashion industry. The most important reason being Black Americans need to acquire and maintain these skills for survival. In times of crisis or destitution people need to be able to make their clothing before looking for the aid of other nations.

A common fact that most Americans don't concern themselves with is that the very few people who move and shake behind the scenes are the ones who rake in the most wealth overall. This is because they own and control industries most people take for granted. Some examples are toiletries, food, clothing, stationery, furniture and health and beauty care goods.

These shadow owners aren't on the news, you don't know their names, they aren't famous, they just quietly collect billions of dollars every year because we unconsciously spend all our money with them. This formula was set up this way so the average citizen wouldn't question it and just blindly purchase the product.

Always remember that they continue to be this powerful because our dollars help them operate at full capacity. It's time now that we turn the tables and become the producers and not just the consumers. As we go along in this book, we will see how vital and prosperous it is to sustain ourselves and what it takes to make it happen.

Now that we've covered the essentials of Black American living and how we can independently implement them into our communities, we can focus our sights on other facets of society. Engaging in the sciences, arts, entertainment and sports, transportation, technology, military, finance, textile, social service, politics, renewable energy and green resources and much more.

purchase the product.

Section 5:

Science & Technology

Having an active scientific community in your nation is crucial and vital to the progression of the people who live in it. As stated in the Education section, having our scientists, of every discipline, study, and experiment what they find allows us to make advancements as a people. Advancements like finding new species and organisms that exist, inventing and producing new technologies to enhance everyday life, discovering ancient relics and knowledge, uncovering the mysteries of the universe and curing diseases, just to name a few.

One of the first things we need are laboratories and facilities to conduct these experiments. If Black Americans use just five percent (5%) of the yearly expenditure at fifty billion dollars ($50,000,000,000), we will be able to build approximately 1,250 science compounds similar to the Euler Science Complex at Taylor University in Upland, Indiana. If we use the Euler Complex as an example of what's possible, within those 1,250 buildings, Black Americans will have had built 27,500 laboratories and 13,750 classrooms nationwide.

Once inside and operating in these institutions, the possibilities of what can be achieved are endless. Of course, this is an exaggerated example, using the entire budget on these buildings, but once the budget is divided among several different programs, Black Americans will have the facilities necessary for scientific exploration.

Scientific and mathematic intelligence has been used against the black masses across the world for millennia even though historically blacks have been the cultivators of those sciences. Scientists like Benjamin Banneker who invented America's first functional clock after taking a man's watch apart and studying its components. Ophthalmologist Dr. Patricia Bath who invented the Laserphaco Probe, a device that helps remove cataracts lenses. Dr. Daniel Hale who was the pioneer of open heart surgery. Dr. Mae C. Jemison, the first black woman to travel to space in 1992.

Black Americans have been making major headway in the sciences for generations, usually in whited owned facilities and institutions. While Black American scientists could study, research, invent, and master their crafts they were ultimately hindered because of the lack of black owned laboratories to work in. The Patent Act of 1793 and 1836 denied Black Americans the ability to obtain patents for their inventions because they were considered slaves and not citizens. Still, I wonder why there aren't as many Black American scientists out there today.

As I was researching for this section, I noticed that most of the distinguished Black American scientists and inventors were most prominent in the late 1800's to late 1900's. In an era where racism and all the systematic and violent conditions that came with it was at its peak, Black American scientists were making groundbreaking discoveries in various fields of science and inventing industry changing machinery. I believe that as time went on the sciences became less relevant to Black Americans, decreasing the number of young people interested in pursuing these fields of expertise.

In her Wall Street Journal article *"Why Aren't There More Black Scientists?"* Gail Heriot argues that Affirmative Action has ultimately hindered and discouraged Black American college students from pursuing majors in science and engineering. That because colleges are adjusting their academic standards for admission via race and ethnicity, black students who have an interest in STEM (Science, Technology, Engineering and Mathematics) majors often transfer to different majors after their first year because they were not academically prepared for the workload.

Per the Center on Education and the Workforce at Georgetown University, ***"African Americans account for only 8 percent of general engineering majors, 7 percent of mathematics majors, and only 5 percent of computer engineering majors."*** Additionally, five percent (5%) for Mathematics & Statistics, twelve percent (12%) for Computer & Information Sciences and five percent (5%) for Physical Science & Science Technologies.

If that wasn't striking enough, in contrast, our white counterparts' statistics reports an almost complete opposite turnout. According to the National Center for Educational Statistics, sixty-six percent (66.3%) of white college students are awarded degrees in STEM majors. sixty-five percent (65%) for Mathematics & Statistics, sixty-two percent (62%) for Computer & Information

Sciences and seventy percent (70%) for Physical Science & Science Technology.

However, when we zoom in on these Black American STEM graduates we see something that I've always believed and of course encouraged in the Education section of this book. A study from the Department of Education reports that ***"Even though our nation's [Historically Black Colleges and Universities] make up just 3 percent of colleges and universities, they produce 27 percent of African-American students with bachelor's degrees in STEM fields."***

Heriot validates these statistics further in her WSJ article reporting ***"It is no fluke that historically black colleges and universities, or HBCUs, have an excellent record of graduating future scientists and engineers. In 2006 HBCUs accounted for 21% of the bachelor's degrees awarded to black students. Yet 33% of the black students awarded Ph.D.'s in science or***

engineering had received their bachelor's degree at an HBCU.

Probably the single most important reason is that at HBCUs, half the black students have entering credentials in the top half of the class. At competitive colleges elsewhere, given race-preferential admissions, black student credentials cluster at the bottom."

When I read these reports and statistics, I don't get discouraged. Instead I, of course, get inspired. What all this means to me is the point I drove home in the Education section; Black American students learn and achieve more when taught by Black American teachers and professors. The results speak for themselves.

This doesn't discredit the ability for other ethnic groups to teach black students, it's to highlight the importance of having a strong educational presence in our communities. We must look at this data and use it to “up the ante” in the many fields of STEM studies.

Practicing and aspiring Black American STEM graduates in the twenty-first century can meet and surpass their predecessors once we reestablish the importance of science and build and run the facilities to conduct the work. As we can see it is a statistical fact that black colleges and universities produce high performing black scientists, engineers, and mathematicians.

The Black American Scientific Community is another vital piece to the advancement of our people. The world will now be able to refer to case studies made from our labs and institutions by Black American scientists. Our researchers will be able to conduct on-site and in-lab experiments.

Black American biologists and biochemists will be able to provide data on the science of Black American biology. Black American genealogists will be able to provide data showing a person’s family history. Black American engineers will have the tools and materials necessary to create innovative technologies and inventions that will change the world. Our scientific community will positively improve the lives of people nationwide, even worldwide.

In an era where people can access infinite amounts of information from a device that fits inside of their pocket, excelling in science and technology should be a top priority for Black Americans. Technology is the way of the future; this is evident based on how technology is increasingly integrating into our daily routines.

Devices like FitBit activity trackers and GoPro portable HD cameras are a part of our daily lives. Smartphone and computer usage are at an all-time high. Black Americans spend fifteen percent (15%) more time on smartphones than the rest of the American population.

Technology is all around us and available to be used and improved. Instead of just consuming and using this technology, Black Americans will be participating in the creating and manufacturing process of these devices as well. As we've seen in the previous section, having buildings in place to facilitate production is critical. People will be able to use Black American science complexes and factories to invent new technologies that work toward everyone's benefit.

Being able to produce technologies gives Black American the competitive edge in the markets as well. We will no longer have to wait for other companies and nations to release the newest gadget; Black Americans will be releasing devices that meet and exceed the quality of our commercial competitors. Believe it or not, Black Americans have the power and ingenuity to create smartphones that will compete with Apple and Samsung. Black Americans can build renewable energy based technologies that will help replenish planet earth that will compete with General Electric.

History has painted a very vivid picture of Black American innovation and intelligence in the sciences. Black American men and women worked their entire lives to master their crafts, inventing a wealth of knowledge and technology we still use today. Because of this, I know Black American people today will take what our ancestors did (with the limited resources they were afforded) and take it to new heights, and even challenge already established studies.

It is time now for us to take a closer second look at what was taught to be fact within American academia. We must challenge all findings and see if they are held up as accurate and up to date as scientific data. Black Americans and Americans, in general, have been conditioned to accept the results of scientific institutions at face value without any fact checking of their own. This is due to the mass ignorance the American population has when it comes to the sciences.

When an athlete's rankings are reported, saying that he or she is the best or worst in their respected leagues in their respected position, there is an abundance of sports enthusiasts, sports writers and sports analysts that cross reference the data to see if those rankings hold up and are fact, likewise for any other industry that records data.

The Black American population must master this practice in their respected fields to ensure all the things they teach are founded upon scientific evidence and not just the word of the scientist.

Once Black America solidifies our scientific community, we will see a great change in the reception to STEM education from the youth to the adults. Making science and technology a "cool" field to pursue makes it easier for future growth and development. When Black American children see more scientists, engineers, and mathematicians in their community, the more appealing those professions look to them. Once it becomes “cool” to become scientists, we will see a lot more of them popping up in the black community.

Section 6: Entertainment

The entertainment industry thrives off black talent and consumers. The Nielsen Company reports ***"The mean number of annual African-American movie ticket purchases is about 19% higher at 3.7 versus 3.1 for non-Hispanic Whites. Video/PC game store purchases are 71% higher and amusement park purchases are 25% higher than non-Hispanic Whites as well. As the number of higher-income Black consumers continue to grow, purchasing rates will follow suit."***

"In fact, African-American celebrities are among the most well-known, influential marketable personalities and trendsetters across the entire entertainment landscape. In music, Beyoncé is one of three top trendsetting artists in all of the pop genre. Will Smith is the third most widely recognized actor working in the film

industry. Oprah Winfrey is viewed as the most influential media personality in television. And Michael Jordan, one of the most accomplished athletes of all time, is the highest marketable celebrity in all of sports."

According to Statista in 2015, the entertainment and media market in the United States were expected to be worth over $594 billion U.S. dollars ($594,000,000,000) and scheduled to reach over $723.4 billion ($723,400,000,000) by 2019. When we combine these facts, we can conclude that the Black American population is mainly funding yet another industry they don't own, that makes the bulk of their revenue from black talents.

To compete with the big companies that produce media, Black Americans must create their own entertainment industry that caters to the talent, the fan as well as the executive respectively. Black executives are now able to set up and run powerhouse record labels and film studios that rival

Universal and Sony. These companies will be able to make groundbreaking epic films with A-list talents as well as the up and coming, complete with the proper funding to make sure they are created with the highest quality and with state of the art technology.

The Dalian Wanda Group Co Ltd, China's largest private property developer, recently purchased Hollywood film studio Legendary Entertainment for three and a half billion dollars ($3,500,000,000) in January 2016. You may be familiar with Legendary's work like The Dark Knight trilogy, Inception, and Interstellar.

If we use this as an example, we can see that even an established film studio is easily attainable with focused funds from the Black American annual budget. We can also own property developing companies like Dalian that buys businesses to expand their global reach.

Per the Nielsen Company: ***"A full 91% of all African-Americans, or 31 million, listen to the radio weekly. Blacks listen to more radio than the total population at all age levels, particularly in the youngest and the Boomer age ranges: 12-17 (+11% more) and 50-64 (+9% more). Blacks also listen to the radio more than any race or ethnic group, at over 60 hours per month."***

Contrary to popular belief, radio is still a very popular medium used to reach the masses. In present times internet radio and podcasts are an ever-growing industry and because Black Americans are the largest listener base it only makes sense that we control these mediums so we can use them for our economic, musical and informational development.

It is relatively simple to create and start a full-power FM radio station once you have the funding to purchase the proper systems, plants and equipment. We can also buyout already established radio stations that are willing to sell. The cost for a

Class C Radio Transmission System, the highest quality and frequency is approximate $1.2 million dollars each, roughly $60-62.4 million dollars nationwide.

The cost for the necessary radio equipment is about $150,000 each studio. The average cost to buy or construct a 3,000-square foot building to facilitate the radio station is approximate $150,000. Another option is to purchase or build a network building or complex where it houses several radio and TV stations inside of it. This allows us to save developmental land and space by combining the channels together similar to the way other networks operate.

The estimated revenue of U.S radio broadcasters is eighteen billion dollars ($18,130,000,000), an estimated expense of fourteen billion dollars ($14,060,000,000) which makes an estimated profit of about four billion ($4,070,000,000). This is largely due to the relationship broadcasters have with advertisers.

Sixty percent (60%) of American radio listeners say they trust the companies that are advertised over the airwaves.

Local black owned businesses can advertise their companies consistently over the radio. Imagine how much more traffic your business will incur because it is being advertised throughout the day on people's favorite stations. In this aspect of the industry, having a healthy relationship between the broadcasters and advertisers is proven to increase the profitability of any given business.

A great example of this model is the partnership between the black owned internet radio stations Loud Speakers Network and the black owned grooming and personal care business Bevel. The podcasts under the Loud Speakers Network give audible advertisements about Bevel and in return Bevel offers a discount for all the listeners who purchase the shaving kit via a promo code. These types of partnerships are encouraged throughout every industry mentioned in this book because it amplifies the audience for two or more brands at one time, increasing profits for all parties involved.

Creating black owned record labels is a vital piece in the development of black music in this country. It is a fact that black-created music genres have been co-opted and stolen over the ages, Jazz and Rock N' Roll being the most famous examples.

This was due to the lack of constant and total ownership in Black American music by Black Americans. Black talents signed contracts to white owned record companies which allowed those companies to make the rules on who gets paid and credited for the work. Over time white people could mimic the sound and use it to their advantage to the point that allowed them to say they started the genre(s).

When we solidify our own record companies, the music and the artists who make it will forever be recognized as the actual creators, and not the people who heard the sound and ran with it. Another advantage of owning our own record labels is payment and distribution.

In today's climate, because of the internet it is not as hard to become famous without the help of a record label backing you. In time before the web, artists had to shop their music to various radio stations and record labels to be heard by a larger audience. Artists are now able to simply upload their art to a variety of streaming services like Apple Music, Sound Cloud, Band Camp, Audio Mack, etc. from the comfort of their own homes. Artists can reach millions of potential fans from their own virtual spaces and have been doing so without the support of a record label for some time now.

What attracts an up and coming artist to sign with a major record company is that label's ability to give them a lump sum of capital (often called an advance), put their music in public retail spaces like

F.Y.E and Target, radio play, and booking live performance venues.

The problem with this seemingly innocent scenario is that a lot of artists find themselves in debt to the record labels after a while and must conform to what the record label wants them to do to reconcile that debt. This usually means the artist has to make music they aren't passionate about, promote businesses and corporations they would never support and/or even tolerate disrespect from the labels just because they owe them money.

Black owned record companies can now offer artists similar deals without having to sacrifice the integrity and dignity of the artist or put them in bad debt. Black Americans having control over the radio and music retail spaces will ultimately make sentiments like *"this type of music isn't marketable"* null and void.

All our favorite Indie and major music artists can sell their art without selling their soul because they are being pushed by ethical companies who know the real worth of their artists and have the reach to put them in front of the world stage.

Video and PC Gaming is another big entertainment industry that Black Americans can take advantage of economically once we start building and creating companies in that field. Over 150 million people in this country play video games on a regular basis, and as previously stated, Black Americans spend the bulk of the money made in the industry.

Per the Entertainment Software Association in 2014 the total amount consumers spent on video games added up to over $22.4 billion dollars ($22,410,000,000). Other statistically based websites like Statista have reported $27.5 billion dollars ($27,500,000,000) in 2015 and projected to reach $29 billion dollars ($29,000,000,000) in 2016.

The best way for Black Americans to take the gaming industry (or any industry) by storm is to breakdown the technology that fuels it. We must learn and understand what the technology does, how it is made, how it can be improved upon among other technological advances. Building gaming studios is obviously a vital piece in making these discoveries and of course it is possible with the Black American annual budget backing our endeavors.

It costs an estimated three hundred and thirty-one dollars ($331) for Microsoft to build an XBOX One. Twenty-three dollars for the Hard Drive, twenty-six dollars for the Blu Ray Drive, seven dollars for Connectivity, five dollars for Non-Volatile Memory, thirty-nine dollars for Volatile Memory, one hundred and thirty-two dollars for Processors, one dollar for Other ICs, eighteen dollars for Power Management and Audio, twenty-nine dollars for Housings and Mechanicals, thirty dollars for Miscellaneous Items, four dollars for Supporting Materials and seventeen dollars for Final Assembly and Test.

When we build our own gaming studios, not only can we bring the latest and greatest video games to the global market, but also the gaming consoles they are played on. With some light research, we will discover that there are dozens of black owned game developers like Black Division Games, a Kenyan interactive entertainment and publishing company. Black Division Games created the very first African First Person Shooter Multiplayer video game in the world.

Another example would be Nerjyzed Entertainment, the first African-American development studio to ship content onto next-generation consoles. Nerjyzed released *"BCFx: The Black College Football Xperience"* in 2009, the only black college football video game in existence.

Electronic Arts, Inc. (EA Sports) reported $4.52 billion dollars ($4,520,000,000) in revenue in 2015. In May of 1982, EA's Founder Trip Hawkins called for a meeting with a man by the name of Don Valentine, founder of the venture capital firm

Sequoia Capital. In the meeting, Hawkins proposed that Valentine invest in his then named company *"Amazin' Software."*

At the time, Hawkins was working for Apple as the Director of Product Marketing. Hawkins left Apple and started his company in a spare office at Sequoia. Seven months after Hawkins changed and incorporated the name "Electronic Arts, Inc." with a personal investment of two hundred thousand dollars ($200,000) he secured several investments from venture capital firms including Sequoia Capital which summed up to a total of two million dollars ($2,000,000), adjusted for inflation a little under five million dollars ($4,958,777).

When Black Americans start investing their funds in companies like Black Division Games and Nerjyzed Entertainment we give them the ability to keep creating better content as time goes by just like EA, Inc. Most people don't realize that they can build and create their wants and needs and not just be complacent in consuming them. We have the capacity to manifest whatever it is we desire, all people need are the resources, and it is a statistical fact that we have them.

These principles have been practiced for centuries in the United States and because Black Americans spend so much wealth it is easy to conclude that when they start using these methods of investment for themselves, the outcome will reach above and beyond what other groups have produced.

Technology is at the forefront of all human advancement, whether for entertainment or utility. So, when the Black American population takes control of the technology, we will be the ones placing the newest products in the public eye and then the marketplace.

Section 7: Sports

It is a well-known fact that Black Americans and sports go together like peanut butter and jelly in society. For generations, Black Americans have participated in the variety of sports teams and leagues in the United States, and when we focus our economy and talent to dominate the industry, we will see just how powerful the black presence in sports is.

When the average American thinks about sports they often think of their favorite team or player. Even more often, those teams are predominantly made up of black people. From LeBron James to Tiger Woods, from Serena Williams to Gabrielle Douglas, black people have been the shining stars in most sports in this country since they've been playing them.

Per Plunkett Research, Ltd, the US Sports industry in the year and season of 2015 raked in a little under five billion dollars ($498,400,000,000) in revenue, globally at one and a half trillion dollars ($1,500,000,000,000). If Black American athletes were to stop playing for these already established leagues and teams, the resulting loss in profit would be devastating to the entire sports industry.

Without the black talent, the games aren't as enjoyable to be a part of and watched. The driving force to keep fans in stadium seats and watching on the television is the level of athleticism these players display in the game, and historically black men have been the primary seat fillers.

Just imagine if all your favorite black athletes stopped playing for the teams they are a part of, would you keep watching on a weekly basis? Would you still have the same affinity for the team or the league when you don't see the black athletes you're used to? I highly doubt it.

In the documentary *"7 A.M"*, a film about the power of the black dollar in the United States, it details a time where the Negro Sports Leagues were the crown jewel in the black community. Black athletes trained hard to be a part of the Negro Leagues because, in the days of segregation, it was against the law to play in white owned leagues.

Athletes like Jackie Robinson, Hank Aaron, and Satchel Paige were the prime examples of what we consider superstars in the industry. What brought about the breakdown of the black owned teams and leagues was the illusion that white owned teams and leagues were a better institution. The black community went from glorifying the Negro Leagues to being conditioned to encourage their favorite athletes to abandon the black owned teams and leagues to be a part of the white owned ones.

This is an economic strategy that has been used for generations in this country. The dominant society advertises and promotes their way of thinking and living to others which subconsciously conditions the masses to believe that they are perceivably better than every other group and we should aspire to live and think like them.

We have been told that nothing is of substantive significance if it is not validated by a white man or woman. It is so ingrained in the minds of blacks to seek this validation that many aren't aware that they do it.

For example, if a young black man or woman decides to educate their friends and family on things pertaining to their health and nutrition, their peers will be less likely to accept the information as fact because they don't fit the description of what they have been taught a knowledgeable person on health should look like.

The information is usually just as valid and in a lot of cases contradicts the Western doctrine, showing what they've once believed to be untrue. Still, because they have been conditioned to take heed to the Western doctrine, those young men and women are discredited as giving false information. This is what happened with sports in Black America, and it is time now for us to capitalize on the industry on an institutional level and not just as players and coaches.

Black Americans can create their own stadiums, leagues, and teams that the masses can participate in. First, we must create our own leagues in all sports. Basketball, Football, Baseball, Soccer, Hockey, etc. For the sake of this book, we will call them the Independent Leagues, respectively to each sport (i.e. Independent Baseball League or Independent Basketball League).

One thing that has been talked about in barbershops across the country is the possibility of retired players creating and/or coaching their own teams, hiring staff and players to allow the youth a higher chance of becoming a career athlete. This is an excellent idea.

When superstars like LeBron James, Kevin Durant, Carmelo Anthony and Stephen Curry retire they will be able to own teams in the Independent Basketball League. The young basketball players that grew up watching them play will love working for their organizations. I'm even willing to predict that more young athletes will want to play for the Independent Leagues over the National Leagues because we will have the star power on our side.

The youth of today are bitter sweetly highly influenced by entertainment, popular culture and sports to the degree that young aspiring athletes see themselves in their favorite players' game. I say bitter sweetly because while it is great that children have adult entertainers and athletes they can watch and enjoy, there are some unhealthy behaviors associated with the fandom that negatively affects the youth. Children should have heroes, let's just make sure they are people that they could learn from.

The average worth of a franchise in the NBA is about one and a quarter billion dollars ($1,250,000,000). This is because the franchise owners make sponsorship agreements with large corporations like PepsiCo, Verizon, and Nike.

Sponsorship and endorsement deals bring in the most revenue for these teams because they're able to sell promotions and advertisements to the consumers that watch the games.

In the 2014-2015 season sponsorship spending topped at seven hundred and thirty-nine million dollars ($739,000,000). There is a deal in place that will have the corporate sponsors logos stitched onto the NBA player's jerseys in the 2017-2018 season. When the Independent Leagues form partnerships with black owned businesses and corporations, the outcome will match and even exceed the results of the status quo.

The next phase of this initiative is to solidify venues for the Independent Leagues to play in. Black Americans can build stadiums like the newly constructed Barclays Center in Brooklyn, New York or we can rent out pre-existing stadiums like Madison Square Garden in New York City or the Staples Center in Los Angeles, California. In the same way the black owned record companies will be able to afford to put their artists in these venues, the black owned leagues will as well.

Per Athletic Business Media, Inc. ***"The three newest pro football stadiums have cost $720 million (Lucas Oil Stadium, 2008), $1.15 billion (Cowboys Stadium, 2009) and $1.6 billion (MetLife Stadium, 2010). Major League Baseball hasn't seen quite that level of inflation, but it has produced the three most expensive ballparks in history in 2008 (Nationals Park, $611 million) and 2009 (Citi Field, $900 million; Yankee Stadium, $1.5 billion)."*** With the hundreds of millions of dollars that these National athletes make alone, Black Americans could start to build their own stadiums.

It took one billion dollars ($1,000,000,000) for The Barclays Center to be constructed. If we used the Barclays Center's costs for construction as a base for stadiums, Black Americans would be able to buy 1,000 stadiums nationwide. Luckily there isn't a need for that many. Cutting the number down to 25 or less and still have more than nine hundred billion dollars ($975,000,000,000) or more to use for other endeavors would be the best solution.

The athletes under the Independent Leagues will be paid just like any other league. I even propose we pay the student athletes on the University and Collegiate levels as well. The National Collegiate Athletic Association (NCAA) brought in a little under a billion dollars at nine hundred million dollars ($912,300,000) in 2015, and none of it went to the student athletes' pockets.

Since the sponsorships and advertisements would be virtually useless without the players filling the seats and keeping the televisions tuned in, I propose we pay our student athletes a living salary they can also use to pay off any loans they may incur or build wealth while enrolled in school.

A known fact for black student athletes is that a lot of them are hoping and working for a chance to make it to the big leagues. A big reason for that is economically based. Young black student athletes grow up struggling financially and bank on their athleticism to save them and their families from a life of poverty. Student athletes, especially the top ranking, are generally excused from their academic responsibilities to fulfill their duties on the field or court.

This promotes to the athlete that education isn't as important as sports and they usually behave accordingly, their grades show it. So, you have poverty stricken athletes that aren't performing the way they should be in classrooms because they are worried about making sure their families don't struggle.

The solution to this dilemma is to pay the student athletes. Once our athletes are making a living wage, they can now devote equal attention to their athleticism as well as their schoolwork. When we support our local businesses, families won't have to live in poverty because our communities will be thriving.

This means that students won't have the pressure of "saving" their family while away at school. Receiving income from their occupation, having supportive households in the community coupled with the best educational facilities in the country gives the student athlete the opportunity to excel in other areas of their collegiate careers that don't deal with sports. Once we apply these basic principles to the sports industry, we will see an enormous change in the status quo and a more prosperous endeavor for all those involved.

Section 8: Transportation

Per the American Public Transportation Association ***"In 2011, total public transit expenditures were $55.4 billion, with $38.4 billion spent for operations and $17.1 billion spent on capital investments. Heavy rail investments are the largest modal capital expenditures, at $5.5 billion, followed by bus capital investments, at $4.7 billion. The largest type of capital investment was for guideways, at $5.4 billion, followed by vehicles, at $4.7 billion."***

Public transportation is another industry that most American citizens take for granted. Yes, millions of people rely on this mode of transport, but not many know what goes into making this industry function the way it does.

Mass transit has traditionally been funded by institutional subsidies provided by the local and national government (via the taxes on gas and automobiles), advertisements and fares. While there are some benefits to operating your businesses through government subsidies that we should take advantage of, I still believe that Black Americans should stick to their private endeavors until we can penetrate the various facets of government. This way Black Americans can establish conducive political positions that will push legislation that is going to work to our benefit.

It would be a better idea that Black Americans pool their monies together to purchase and operate our own public transportation systems throughout the United States instead of solely relying on the government to provide funding.

I know what you may be thinking *"We already have public transportation in our cities. How on earth could we create our own mass transit businesses?"* The answer is quite simple. Just like various college campuses around the country who provide public transport for their students and staff,

Black Americans will begin in small areas, preferably sectors that are underserved and expand those routes to broader places. For the sake of this book, we will call the transportation system the "Independent Public Transit Authority" or "IPTA."

In application, the IPTA will provide service for people who live in communities that don't have efficient public transportation available to them. The IPTA will map out routes that are conducive to the individuals who ride the vehicles, considering their behaviors and job location(s). So, if a large number of a community lives on Main Street, works on Broad Street and shops on Elm Street, the IPTA will provide routes that cater to those behaviors to ensure the community gets to and from these locations in the most efficient ways possible.

With just one hundred billion dollars ($100,000,000,000) or ten percent (10%) of the Black American annual budget, we can run and operate our own public transportation systems. In Uganda, Africa, the Kiira Motor Company has built

Africa's first line of solar and electric powered buses. Named the Kayoola, the bus will create no fumes that will harm the environment as well as employ thousands of Ugandans to help maintain the motor company. The production costs to build a Kayoola is about $58,000 each. If the IPTA uses ten billion dollars ($10,000,000,000) out of the Transportation budget, it will be able to build over one hundred thousand buses (100,000) nationwide.

Businesses like the IPTA are mainly dependent on the participation of the community. The more people that ride these methods of independent public transport, the more the company will expand and flourish. However, when the people don't patronize these businesses, the businesses will inevitably fail. Even though this applies to the IPTA, this principle applies to all firms in the community. Consistent and constant patronage is critical.

This initiative isn't exclusive to buses either, trolley and train systems are also viable forms of mass transit that Black Americans can create and utilize for the greater good of the community. Historically the use of the trolley or the "streetcar" was one of the best methods of transportation in an ever growing nineteenth century America. The mode was fueled by horse or electricity and connected communities, cities and states.

Through a myriad of factors like suffering labor relations, legislation, corporate monopolization and a growing population that became harder to service, streetcars almost entirely vanished from public use. The railcar industry could revive itself in the twenty first century by learning from the mistakes of the past.

Instead of fighting for the road, buses and trolleys can share the streets in a harmonious system of public transport. In areas that have wide streets that are best suited for larger vehicles, we can use the solar and electric powered buses. Similar to the city of San Francisco, California, in areas that have narrower streets and blocks we can use the solar and electric trolleys or cable cars.

Building train systems are something Black Americans can achieve as well. Purchasing land throughout the communities and building railroad tracks will open a cleaner, more efficient way to travel within the areas. Just like every other mode of public transit, the train system will be electric and solar powered to ensure the least environmental impact on the planet. Trains will run throughout the cities at first and will expand to larger routes, connecting other cities and states. The IPTA's train system will be able to connect businesses in other areas by allowing them to trade goods back and forth through the railways.

We can rebuild our communities' infrastructure like paving new roads and railways for the IPTA to run as efficiently as possible. Not only does the reconstruction of our infrastructure help secure the operations of the transportation systems, but it also cleans up the communities in the process. Roads that were covered in potholes and craters can be fixed along with newly painted traffic lines.

New lanes can be made for private vehicles like automobiles, motorcycles and bicycles as well as public transport like buses, and trolleys. Street lights and signs can be restored. As I have already stated, when the environment is clean, the residents are more likely to maintain the environment's cleanliness.

Public transportation is the answer to the congestion on the roads in major and minor cities in this country. We can improve the systems that we are familiar with in our own facilities. As someone who uses both public and private transportation I have assessed the following:

- Private transportation is just that, private and riders have the freedom to travel in any way that they please.

- Public transportation saves passengers time and money when traveling.
- Private transportation is the primary cause of the congestion on the roads.
- Public transportation systems have been stagnant and do not cater to the modern passenger. No proper areas for storage.

Because people have the right to travel about the country, and by extension the world, I encourage private transportation. I enjoy road trips and driving in the countryside of places or just driving around the city. I am not against private transportation at all; I am suggesting that we keep it to a minimum in highly concentrated areas.

These areas are better suited for efficient public transportation systems that will decrease the density of traffic as well as reduce the amount of pollution that comes because of CO2 emissions from the automobiles. If we are going to use private transportation in these congested areas I propose we only use them for necessity or emergency.

In this case, theoretically, if you live in a city and work downtown of that city, instead of driving to work you would use the IPTA system. However, if you lived in the city and worked in the suburbs (or vice versa), I can understand the necessity of private transportation. Still, it is not difficult to connect the cities to their suburban counterparts through the IPTA systems and should be encouraged and used whenever possible.

The biggest problem out of the ones I listed is the current systems of public transport's inability to cater to new day passengers. Trains and buses are crowded with no leg room, are often late, unsanitary, with a lack of storage space and sometimes even harmful to the passengers.

All these problems can be fixed with a newer and better system. The IPTA will cater to the modern-day passenger by making sure the vehicles have enough room to seat passengers comfortably. The IPTA will provide ample room for storage of passenger belongings onboard. The IPTA will create routes that will satisfy the travelers' needs and wants when it comes to accessibility to their community at the best times and schedules.

The IPTA will provide top tier customer service from all operators and staff members. The IPTA will be an environmentally friendly business that will use renewable energy and resources to help promote the importance of properly integrating Mother Nature and industry. The goal of the IPTA is to make it an easy choice when faced with the decision of whether you should take your car for the day and bring a balance between public and private transportation.

Now that we understand what a proper transit system can do for any given community, we can start detailing with how Black Americans can focus their skills on getting into the manufacturing of automobiles for private transport. The same Ugandan company mentioned previously; the Kiira Motor Company will be manufacturing private cars as well. Kiira Motors' factory will be settled on one hundred acres, employ two thousand people and produce sixty thousand vehicles a year. KMC will start production in 2018 and will include SUVs, Trucks, the Kayoola, the SMACK and Pick-Ups.

As we can see, building and operating Black owned motor companies is not a difficult task once we start peeling back the layers of the industry and understanding the process of making it a reality, but we still must be aware of the pitfalls that can and have happened in the past.

As I was researching motor companies that were started in the American automotive industry in recent years, I noticed several car companies that met their demise not too long after they began. An example of this misfortune was American-based car company Fisker Automotives, Inc. (now known as Karma Automotives, LLC.). After only 6 years of operation, Fisker declared bankruptcy in 2013 and was bought out by Chinese automotive components manufacturer Wanxiang Group Corporation. Something that I expected when reading how Fisker went under was the problem being rooted in economics.

Fisker received loans totaling over five hundred million dollars ($528,700,000) from the Department of Energy. Because the loans were provided by the state and federal government, they were able to put a freeze on Fisker's credit line when the company failed to reach the agreed conditions for the loans. This resulted in Fisker seeking out financing elsewhere.

In 2012 Fisker secured over three hundred million dollars ($392,000,000) in funding from several different investors. Per The Wall Street Journal, Fisker raised more than one billion dollars ($1,000,000,000) in equity and by 2013 had to lay off seventy-five percent (75%) of their workforce without notice because they couldn't find new investors. They were officially bought out in 2014 by Wanxiang for a little over one hundred and forty-nine million dollars ($149,200,000) in an auction after another Chinese corporation, Hybrid

Technology, LLC purchased Fisker's defaulted government loans.

We can take away several lessons from Fisker's story, the biggest one being using private funds to start, operate and run our automotive companies instead of accumulating loans from the government. Our automotive manufacturers will be privately funded through investments from the Transportation Budget stated at the beginning of this section.

According to Tesla Motor, Inc.'s Annual Report of 2015 they brought in four billion dollars ($4,050,000,000) in Sales and Revenue with the Cost of Goods (COGS) at three billion dollars ($3,120,000,000) which sets their gross profit at over nine hundred million dollars ($923,500,000).

Investing ten billion dollars ($10,000,000,000) in a black owned car manufacturing company would cover all operating costs while also allowing for the future development of the enterprise without the hassle of external forces controlling the processes. To keep our transportation section consistent with all the other modes of transport we will produce cars that are electric and solar powered as well.

Maintaining this principle is very important because of how detrimental gasoline powered cars have become to the overall health of planet earth. While we want to make headway in all facets of industry, we also want to ensure we have a place to call home at the end of the day. If doing your job meant that it would damage and ultimately destroy your house, you wouldn't participate. At least I hope you wouldn't.

Too many factories around the world are unnecessarily polluting the earth and when we build our facilities we will make sure to use environmentally friendly materials. Likewise, the already established factories we buyout.

We will update and renovate each facility to ensure it is up to par with the standards we set in the industry. The goal is to replace the old technology with the new so we can properly sustain our businesses and livelihoods.

Black America needs to penetrate the airline industry just as much as the other forms of transport. Air travel is another one of those industries that we as Americans take for granted. We buy our tickets and pay the fees, but barely ever think to own and operate our own airlines and airports. It is possible to get into the aviation industry; all it takes is the research and capital to make it happen. More in-depth research is required and encouraged (as with every other industry mentioned in this book) to put things in motion, but those who are ambitious and adamant enough will use this and put the pieces together with their own due diligence.

In 2015 the International Air Transport Association (IATA) reports ***"The International Air***

Transport Association (IATA) announced its airline industry outlook for 2016 which sees an average net profit margin of 5.1% being generated with total net profits of $36.3 billion. IATA also announced a revision to its airline industry outlook for 2015 upwards to a net profit of $33 billion (4.6% net profit margin) from $29.3 billion forecast in June."

"Revenues are expected to rise by 0.9% to $717 billion in 2016. Industry revenues peaked in 2014 at $758 billion, then declined to $710 billion in 2015 with the impact of the strengthening of the US dollar on non-dollar revenues. The increase in revenues in 2016 is expected to be wholly due to the contribution of the passenger side of the business ($525 billion in 2015 rising to $533 billion in 2016)."

Still within the Transportation Budget, Black Americans can invest ten billion dollars ($10,000,000,000) in a black owned airline. For the sake of this piece, we will call the airline,

IndependentAir. We have the option of being an LCC (Low Cost Carrier) or a Full-Service Carrier. Most airlines that we are familiar with are LCC's so that's where this piece will put its focus on. IndependentAir will not only be in airports across the world providing passage to destinations known and unknown, but they will also manufacture their own planes and airports as well.

The cost to purchase a commercial airplane, specifically the Boeing 737-700 is approximately seventy-eight million dollars ($78,300,000) each. This, of course, is the MSRP or Manufacturer's Suggested Retail Price that applies mostly to private consumers, but when airlines are seeking to purchase a fleet of aircrafts for their business, the cost can be cut up to half the price during negotiations. This lets us know that building our own airplanes will be most profitable in the long term. By this math, we can conclude the cost is closer to twenty million dollars ($20,000,000) or less to build.

For us to start manufacturing our own aircrafts, we must first build facilities to do so. The Boeing Everett Factory, a 98-acre building (the world's largest by volume) set on 780 acres that house the facilities required to assemble their crafts cost approximately two million dollars ($2,355,600) to purchase the land alone. Since its inception in 1968, the property has expanded to over one thousand acres (1,025).

The entire project totaled at one hundred fifteen million dollars ($115,000,000) and currently employs thirty thousand people, producing seven planes a month. As we already know, that price is just a drop in the bucket to what Black Americans spend every year and we should set our sights on building a factory that is comparable to the giant that Boeing is. I also want to note that Boeing produces rockets, rotorcrafts, and satellites as well.

One of the primary motivations for this initiative came from my last flight with Frontier Airlines. I flew to Detroit, Michigan for New Years and my flight was leaving from Trenton-Mercer Airport, a small airport in Trenton, New Jersey. Trenton-Mercer Airport currently only serves Frontier Airlines and seeing this gave me the idea of researching how possible it is to start an airport with an accompanying airline.

Building an airport isn't cheap, but it is also not impossible or unattainable. The Denver International Airport was built at the cost of almost five billion dollars ($4,800,000,000) and is the largest airport in the United States. Reportedly, because of delays and setbacks early on, the construction was two billion dollars over budget. Still within the Transportation Budget, Black Americans can purchase land and build an airport (that is up to par with the industry's giants) that provides passage across the world.

Investing three billion dollars ($3,000,000,000) per airport into this endeavor will allow Black Americans to successfully acquire more businesses that will influence the global market. There are smaller airports that I can use as an example, but I would much rather put the juggernauts under the microscope so we can see what is currently the leading standard in the industry and what it takes to achieve that status. My version of "starting small" is pursuing the best options for businesses one business at a time.

So, for now, having an airport that rivals the DIA is primary, and then we can build more as the years go on in all applicable cities and states in the country. Having our own airports allows us to not only see the world, but it also encourages the masses that anything is possible.

You may or may not be wondering if the Air travel industry has made any technological advancements in regards to renewable fuels and the answer to your inquiry is yes. Aviation biofuels will be used on all aircrafts for the same reasons that apply to automobiles and trains.

Using biofuels cuts costs and negative environmental impact in the long term. It is imperative that current and aspiring industrialists take heed to the necessity of using environmentally friendly materials for all their endeavors because it assures the future utilization of the industry without worrying about killing the ground it was founded upon.

While we're becoming captains of our own plane, train and automobile industries we can also focus on becoming masters of the seas by building and operating our own ships. Whether it be cruise lines, container ships or personal transport, Black Americans can profit greatly from creating our own businesses that cater to waterway traveling. Starting a Cruise Ship Line, like the other forms of transportation is very doable when we apply our finances and education accordingly. When it comes to cruise ships, you want to carve a niche in why your fleet is better than the household named competitors. From my research, it seems one of the best ways is to start and run several small cruise ship lines as opposed to a few big ones.

Lines like Royal Caribbean and Carnival are the "big boys" of the industry, but what also comes with that is the responsibility of mass producing high quality service to thousands of passengers each voyage. This can become tough over time and will almost inevitably hurt the standard of quality in the company.

When we invest in building cruise lines that carry one hundred to three hundred passenger ships instead of the norm of three thousand we will see an upswing in patronage due to the convenience and exclusivity of each voyage. This cut costs tremendously while also allowing the lines to maintain a standard of safety and quality that shines in comparison to other cruise lines.

Investing five billion dollars ($5,000,000,000) in each cruise line will pay for the insurances, permits, licenses and other expenses that come along with the business. One of the biggest expenses would, of course, be the ships themselves, costing between fifty million to one hundred million dollars ($50,000,000-$100,000,000) each, depending on size and features included on the ships.

Building and/or buying 10 ships would cost up to a billion dollars ($1,000,000,000) and able to carry to up to 3,000 passengers across the entire fleet. For the sake of this piece, we will call the company Freedom Cruise Lines. Freedom will design and follow their own routes, selecting their desired destinations known and unknown.

Freedom will encourage world travel and discovery for all potential riders. By setting sail to the different regions of the world, Freedom will allow passengers the opportunity to embrace different cultures, environments, and people while also being entertained and catered to. Freedom will broaden people's worldview by conducting Continental Tours where ships travel to various countries in Africa, South America, Europe and others.

This initiative doesn't stop at cruise lines; it also includes cargo shipping via container ships. Like I briefly mentioned in the Clothing section, importing materials from other places around the world will serve as a conduit for Black American industry. This is where our shipping containers come in.

I'm more than sure you've seen one of those massive container ships carrying dozens of colorful rectangular metal boxes before in your life. These container ships transport goods and materials back and forth between countries. The average cost for a container ship is about ten million dollars ($10,000,000) each. Still within the Transportation budget, Black Americans can invest five billion dollars ($5,000,000,000) in our own shipping companies and make the trades with other nations easier.

Having our own shipping companies allows us to have access to people and places that may not have been possible before. These ships are the reason we have foreign cars in the United States. These ships are the reason goods and services are cheaper in America. It is true that without proper execution, outsourcing can do more harm than good.

I do not propose we totally outsource jobs from Black America to other countries, but I do suggest that we do business with other nations to optimize the type of goods and services we offer. If a country in South America or Africa has original (transferable) material that would better suit a product we are making domestically, we can negotiate with those countries and then ship the materials to our factories. This way we can keep the jobs domestic while we still build on our international business relations ultimately improving their economies.

Simple practices like this will go a long way in the business realm because of how saturated the industry is with undercutting and exploitive behaviors. When we show ourselves to be honest business people, the world will respond by giving us good business. Of course other facets of independent transportation can and should be considered, I just wanted to detail what one hundred billion dollars, ten percent (10%) of the Black American budget can do when properly applied.

Section 9: Finance

I'm more than sure that reading all these figures of capital has encouraged you and made you happy about what Black Americans can achieve with the money we spend every day; I know I have. However, a truth that was briefly mentioned in the introduction that needs to be addressed in detail is the consistent perpetuation of financial illiteracy in Black America.

Financial illiteracy is why Black Americans spend a trillion dollars a year and don't control any industries. Economic illiteracy is the reason why people are drowning in bad debt and are struggling to get out all while still spending trillions of dollars in their lifetime, collectively. We are conditioned to live above our means and spend money we don't have, usually in the form of credit cards and/or monthly payments and fees.

Being in bad debt is big business for the few people who stand to profit from it, believe it or not. It is time for Black Americans to wise up on how to manage their wealth to come out and avoid bad debt altogether.

First, Black Americans must create a banking system that works for the benefit of the people. There are 21 black owned banks currently in the United States that Black Americans can bank with instead of the institutions we are used to. What many don't know is that banks and other financial institutions are one of the primary reasons you see skyscrapers and schools built in your city. Contractors go to banks and receive grants, investments, and loans to fund their endeavors. This has been practiced in this country for generations and is one of the main driving forces that makes American capitalism thrive.

OneUnited Bank is a black owned and operated bank headquartered in Boston, Massachusetts with branches in Miami, Florida and

Los Angeles, California. As of December 2013, OneUnited Bank has maintained a total of over six hundred and sixteen million dollars ($616,400,000) in total assets.

That may seem like a lot of money (and it is), but for context, Wells Fargo assets total at almost two trillion dollars ($1,787,000,000,000), Bank of America at over two trillion ($2,140,000,000,000), and PNC Bank at three hundred fifty eighty billion dollars ($358,000,000,000). Even though OneUnited is headquartered in Massachusetts, American citizens can enroll and bank with them regardless of the state they live in.

The more people that enroll and open banking accounts at black owned banks, the more assets the bank can acquire which results in the manifestation of all the things mentioned in this book. The cost to start a new bank is about five hundred thousand to one million dollars ($1,000,000) and then up to thirty million dollars

($30,000,000) as backing capital. Most banks are registered as Chartered Financial Institutions (CFIs) that are regulated and supervised under Central Bank Regulation.

I suggest Black Americans start, operate and run our own Non-Bank Financial Institutions (NBCI's) over a CFI because it keeps the overall control of the capital in the private institutions instead of the federal government. As we learned with Fisker in the previous section, the federal government can sometimes seize control of our assets when we rely on them for funding instead of our collective private wealth. This is not to say the government is an evil entity, but to encourage the average citizen to have control over their finances.

Black Americans must implement discernment when making decisions in the finance sector. Just like every other industry in this book, people must do their due diligence, research, test, log results and make decisions accordingly to ensure the outcome works best for those who participate.

Credit Unions are a type of NBCI that is growing in popularity worldwide. Over one hundred million Americans are using Credit Unions over banks and the numbers are expected to increase by two percent (2%) a year. Credit Unions offer virtually all the same services that banks do but with higher interest rates for savings, lower credit card and loan rates and lower fees. There are a lot of advantages to joining Credit Unions and when Black Americans start building them it will help further the security of the wealth staying and maintaining in the community.

Black Americans can use the same amount of capital used to build banks to create credit unions. Our Finance Budget will be one of the largest in this book at thirty-five percent (35%) or more of the Black American annual budget, three hundred and fifty billion dollars ($350,000,000,000). With this much capital, we will be able to build hundreds of financial institutions across the United States.

Our Credit Unions will be able to give out grants, loans, and invest in black owned corporations throughout the country, allowing our private sector to grow and establish themselves in their respective community. This plan also seeks to educate the people on proper wealth management to make sure that as many people as possible know the fundamentals of financial literacy such as tax laws, business laws, corporate laws, budgeting, investing, etc.

Being able to leave behind a sum of wealth to our descendants is imperative to the future of Black Americans, and through these educational tools, we will acquire the wherewithal to apply the practices necessary for continual financial growth.

Starting our own private (and public) stock exchange is another idea I believe Black Americans can benefit from. For the sake of this piece, we will call the exchange the Independent Stock Exchange (ISE). The idea is, business owners put their companies on the ISE and then allow the people to invest in shares of each company, very similar to the way things work on the popular exchanges like the NYSE or NASDAQ. When we do this, it shows what this book is exactly about, group economics.

The more people invest in these businesses; the larger the businesses can become. When this happens, shareholders' wealth rises alongside the company, making it a mutually profitable endeavor for all parties. Companies are then able to pay out dividends to the shareholders, reaffirming their stock positions with them.

Imagine if you owned shares of your favorite black owned clothing brand. Every time you bought a garment from them, it added to your personal wealth. It's like you paid yourself to wear the clothing. You will be more likely to wear the brands, which advertises it to as many people as possible, encouraging them to shop and invest in the company as well.

This is how major brands like Nike and Ralph Lauren operate and it would be nothing but beneficial for Black Americans once they adopt these business principles. This can be a reality for all firms in the community with enough research, participation and backing capital.

A good example of this is the Startup Stock Exchange (SSX). The SSX specifically targets up and coming businesses and allows them a global marketplace to receive investments from people via owning shares of the company. Having a stock exchange centered in Black America will help reinforce the financial independence of the financial institutions we build.

These institutions will securely keep the money we spend every year inside of our communities without the struggle of not knowing how to manage it. We cannot expect everyone to be extremely versed in finance, but we can create environments that put their worries at ease when dealing with their money.

Financial advisors, wealth managers, CPAs, finance lawyers, bankers, etc. are all necessary so investors and consumers can know their real financial power. When a population is economically literate, it prevents and reverses the negative behaviors we've been so used to practicing. Applying for predatory loans, frivolous spending habits, living check-to-check, overwhelming debts, etc. have all been things that plague our finances and have been for a very long time.

Having these professionals in our community will offset these behaviors which will only add to the Black American wealth. The goal is to become a bad debt free nation and implementing these practices and institutions will be able to make that happen in the short and long term.

For Black Americans to stop being perpetually poor, we must build an economic base first and foremost that we can grow from. We must use our money like tools instead of coupons for goods. We must save and invest more than we spend, and when we do spend money, we must spend it with companies inside our communities and with the knowledge that it will make you more money.

There is no other solution to our financial problems in this country, and I encourage everyone reading this book to research and look up black owned businesses that provide the things you want before any other. Whether it be food, clothing, shelter, entertainment, cosmetics, care goods or sports, support black owned companies that provide these products and services first. We must apply discipline and discernment with our money and honestly spend it wisely.

Section 10: Social Services

Our communities desperately need proper social services. For too long our current system of handling social issues has only exacerbated the problems. While seeking solutions to these problems Black American families have been torn apart, destabilization of our communities grew, the lack of peace and unity all have been due to systematic misinformation and malpractice on a social level.

Our communities have seen the worst conditions imaginable in the United States and because of that we owe it to ourselves to completely change what we've been doing. Black American social service should be unique and particular to the problems that we personally face on a day to day basis. High crime rates and violence amongst our people being the most prevalent. Our social programs should be in direct connection to the other sections in this book. It is important that we seek and use viable solutions to our everyday problems.

One of the biggest reasons there is such a high volume of crime and violence in Black American communities is because the men and women do not have productive and positive means to express themselves. When a child is born into an environment that almost completely ensures they will be impoverished for their entire lives, the child tends to behave accordingly and ultimately loses their chance at being a great human being. Too many of Black America's youth are being sent to jail and prison because of bad life decisions, and we must face this problem head on, sooner than later.

Black American parents helplessly live within a system that has been taught to keep them in a perpetual state of grief and misery when it comes to raising their children in this society. One of the biggest, if not the biggest problems Black Americans have is finding decent employment that will allow them to raise their families properly. Therefore, most youths in these situations look to a lifc of crime.

Contrary to mainstream media's perception, black people are not inherently violent criminals. However, when raised in a desperate environment where it is taught that a life of crime is the fastest way to solve that desperation, the people will soon follow suit and almost create a culture around it. From my studies, economics is at the root of these problems, and when we fulfill the duties of the other sections of this piece, we will see a change in our crime and unemployment rates and overall social status as a people.

For starters, Black Americans can build and rebuild their community centers. Through my research, I stumbled upon the concept design of a community center in Fullerton, California. The design was beautiful and had amazing programs to offer. The building has three wings; the Recreation Wing, the Community Service Wing, and the Boys

& Girls Club Wing. The Recreation Wing includes a double gymnasium, a 25-yard indoor pool, fitness rooms and men and women's locker rooms. The Community Service Wing includes offices for staff, computer teaching room, 4,500 square foot multi-purpose meeting room with a full-service kitchen and audio-visual capabilities, classrooms, billiards room, arts and crafts room and senior lounge and library. The Boys and Girls Club wing includes staff offices, large multi-purpose game room, arts and crafts room, technology/homework center and teen lounge.

With just two percent (2%) of the Black American annual budget at twenty billion dollars ($20,000,000,000), we can build programs and institutions in every black community in the United States that help solve the issues aforementioned. Community Centers are the heart of any nation on a social level. Community Centers are the places that gather the people together to brainstorm ideas to solve its problems.

For instance, if there is an issue with drug dealers on the block, the community can come together and work to stop the activity from happening. One resident may suggest jailing the dealers; a business owner may want to hire them so they won't have to sell drugs for money. The community will deliberate and come to a decision and then execute the agreed solution.

Civil togetherness is a major key to maintaining a thriving community or nation. The people must be able to trust their neighbors; the children must be reassured that they will be protected when they are outside. The shop owner needs to know their business won't be robbed or destroyed or vandalized in any way. The list of expectations for a thriving community is large but also very doable, even given the current state of American Black people.

Social change isn't as hard as one would believe, especially if they were living in an area that is highly affected by the current system. All it takes is the concerted effort of the willing to make it happen. More and more our youth are understanding and becoming more aware of the problems that we've been dealing with for centuries, and are hungry for viable solutions. We must teach the coming and current generations the importance of control and ownership, which also embodies self-accountability, responsibility, self-reliance, and self-sufficiency.

The masses gravitate toward what is deemed acceptable or "popular" by the whole, leaving room for certain exceptions and nuances in some cases. For example, what is popular in today's climate of black entertainment are television programs called "Reality Shows." Reality shows are hour-long programming that places black talents in situations that evoke consistent conflict and turmoil for the viewing pleasure of the masses, precisely the black masses.

This type of programming though conveyed as just another form of entertainment, is very influential on how people behave and the perception of the people who watch it. When a person continuously watches this type of programming it normalizes the perceived behavior which in turn makes it acceptable or attractive. This is something we can prove through our daily actions.

When a crawling baby continuously sees their parents walk on their two legs, the child will automatically want to mimic that behavior and walk the same way. The visual of the action makes it easier for the child to learn because it is seen as acceptable or attractive. This type of visual learning doesn't go away as we age, it stays with us because humans never stop absorbing information.

So, the solution must be changing the program or in this case, changing the channel. This isn't to say that Black Americans must stop watching reality shows totally, just not to the point it's one of the biggest conveyors of black entertainment.

When we change the standard of what is deemed the most attractive, we alter the behaviors of the people. On a community level, the willing must unify and mobilize their efforts to encourage change. A collective problem communities have that needs to be fixed the high concentrations of pollution taking over the landscape. Those that are willing, who want a clean environment will come together and clean their community.

With only one hundred million dollars ($100,000,000) Black Americans will be able to start sanitation businesses that will clean the cities and towns across the country. Junk and garbage removal companies don't take much to start. After checking your state's regulations on waste removal, acquire permits and insurances Black Americans will be able to purchase the necessary equipment to operate the business.

If a sanitation company wanted to buy ten garbage trucks which would cover an area of about 5,000 homes, it would cost roughly one and a half million dollars ($1,500,000). Purchasing the same amount of roll-off trucks and roll-off dumpsters would cost about two million dollars ($1,700,000). Buying a building to house this business would cost anywhere between two hundred and fifty thousand ($250,000) and one million dollars ($1,000,000).

The facilities will be able to sort, recycle and properly dispose of the trash while also manufacturing supplies like garbage and recycle bins. Of course, this business will follow the same environmental standards as all the other industries, using renewable energy in every way possible. This initiative also allows our recycling centers to sell their recycled materials to other businesses throughout the community.

With a clean community, we can focus on other social services like family counseling and therapy. The word “trauma” comes up a lot when discussing issues within Black American households.

Abuse of the past and present affect each one of the people that have the grave misfortune of bearing witness to it. Parents that are filled with resentment because they may not have planned to have their child(ren), taking it out on them and creating a dysfunction in their relationships. Children that may act out or misbehave due to the lack of attention, care, or love from the rest their family. A husband and wife who find themselves in a rough patch in their marriage. A misunderstood individual that suffers from a mental illness.

The list can go on and on, but the good thing about these issues is that there are solutions that can be implemented as soon as possible. Building Family Healing Centers would help mend these problems in an efficient, thorough way in the community. Having several teams of professional therapists, counselors and doctors in place to assist families, couples and individuals to resolve their issues will promote a closer family unit and less controversy throughout the community.

For example, willing families will be able to go to a Family Healing Center to resolve a conflict between a child and their parents or between a husband and his wife. These centers will offer executable solutions that families can practice from the safety of their own homes. When families and households start working together toward solutions the behavior will change the environment the families live in as well.

People must understand that the public behavior a community exhibits starts with the behavior exhibited in private, in the home. Most criminals we see in the cities of this country mainly started from a dysfunctional home that fueled their criminal or abusive behavior from an early age. Young men, women, and children are encouraged to participate in harmful behaviors and soon find themselves living a life of crime or degeneracy with no solutions to stop.

Our Family Healing Centers will be able to catch and solve these problems before they become out of control and negatively affect a person's life beyond repair. Investing one million dollars ($1,000,000) in each Family Healing Center will be enough to build and renovate buildings that can facilitate workshops, offices, classrooms, rehabilitation for addicts and people coming from incarceration, and the accompanied staff that will cater to the Black American community.

With a cleaner and closer community, we can set our sights on other aspects of social service like job training. This coincides with the powers of the Community and Healing centers, where the willing residents are looking for a change. We can use our Community Centers to host job fairs and job training seminars that will better equip the people with the skills and tools to perform to the best of their ability.

Every business owner can recruit people to learn how to work for them. Potential employees can gain knowledge in their desired fields without having to go into bad debt to a college or university.

Job creation is paramount to any thriving community. If every registered black owned business had at least one payable employee that would total to over two million jobs. This isn't counting all the potential jobs the sections in this book entails, which in my estimate would be around ten to twenty million.

With an investment of one million dollars ($1,000,000) each, our job training programs will be able to give the people a thorough education on work ethics, productivity, salary and wages, employee rights and skill building. Aspiring welders, carpenters, plumbers and technicians, nurses, entrepreneurs, capitalists, salesmen, inventors, etc. can attend the job training programs and sharpen their skills in their respective trades.

The black owned businesses of the individual trades will delegate representatives that will work and volunteer to teach their trainees how to excel at their craft. This strengthens the working class' morality and economics while also strengthening the businesses they work for. This creates a perpetual state of productivity in the relationship between employees and employers.

An important sentiment that I must convey as a business owner is that being an employee is not a bad thing. The problem with the current state of employment is the improper distribution of wealth accumulated by the companies and the lack of employee benefits.

The large corporations that people looking for a job from aren't paying their employees a suitable living wage even though these companies accumulate tens and hundreds of billions of dollars every fiscal year; with only two million employees at the most like Walmart (2,100,000 employees), but usually in the hundreds and ten-thousands like Starbucks (191,000 employees) and Apple (66,000 employees).

The solution comes in the form of supporting small and local businesses so they can be financially stable enough to employ people seeking jobs. These corporations can hire so many people because of how much money they make. A local business that can maintain a reliable revenue stream of $250,000-$500,000 a year (about $1,400 a day in sales.) they will be able to pay an average employee up to $50,000 a year for their work, depending on the operational costs and other factors.

With that type of average salary, the ordinary worker can sustain a suitable living where they can save and invest their funds in continuing the perpetuation of proper economics and wealth growth. In this instance the employee will be able to store their money in a black owned financial institution, invest their funds in black owned (and other) businesses, including potentially owning shares of the company they work for which can compound in interest over time, adding more personal wealth. This system will create a cyclical stream of revenue for the ordinary working class citizen which can result in the eradication of unlivable poverty.

A happy consequence of this system is the employees that aspire to be business owners themselves can accumulate the necessary capital to do so. An example would be a Sales Associate or Manager working at a clothing store who uses their paychecks to save and invest in their own clothing brand.

The experience they acquire working in the clothing store coupled with the money they earned working and/or granted from a financial institution will provide the aspiring entrepreneur the necessary resources to open their own business. This methodology applies to every industry mentioned in this book.

Now that we have a clean, united and employed community we can move on to more social services like Emergency Departments; Police, Fire, and Medical responders. It is no secret that the relationship between Black Americans and the police is tumultuous, to say the least. In the past few years, we have been made very aware of the problems of bad policing and brutality that affect our communities. Whether it be cases like Michael Brown or Sandra Bland, we have seen the way some police officers abuse their power over the citizens and then the subsequent lack of justice that usually follows.

It is a fact that statistically most police officers do not abuse their authority over the citizens, but it is also a statistical fact that most of those same police officers (84 percent) witnessed fellow officers using excessive force or abusing their position and fifty-two percent (52%) of them say it isn't unusual for those acts to be unreported, per the US Department of Justice.

The reason Black Americans should create their own Police Departments across the country coupled with working in the current departments is first to protect and serve the black communities and creating jobs for civilians. For the sake of this piece, we will call it the Independent Police Union (IPU). Black American police departments will be able to enforce civil order in the community by using tactics that will neutralize conflict, lethal force being a last resort. Our officers will be residents of the communities they serve in, making it easier for them to appeal to other residents while making it harder for them to abuse their power. An abusive officer won't be able to thrive because they will be faced with the people they abuse daily, as opposed to the officers who abuse in the city and live in the suburbs or vice versa.

We do not want to repeat the same bad practices of police brutality so the IPU will provide and perform psychological testing on all recruits to make sure we assess their ability to do their duty while maintaining the required mental status of an officer of the law. These types of tests will be given throughout the entire length of an officer's career. We cannot and will not tolerate any misconduct by our police force, and in the event of misconduct happening, we will respond to it equal to its infraction.

Our police force will undo the malpractices of the "fraternal order" and use those same brother and sisterhood principles to stand up for truth and accountability. Officers will hold themselves and their counterparts accountable for their actions at all times to maintain civil order in the community. We will stop the behaviors of police brutality by policing ourselves and not allowing the abuse any longer.

A big problem that people face in the black community is the disproportionate ratios of white cops patrolling their streets over black ones. This year a man by the name of Alton Sterling was murdered in cold blood by two officers of the Baton Rouge Police Department in Louisiana. The population of Baton Rouge is over fifty percent (50%) black, while the population of their police department is over sixty percent (60%) white.

So, when the police are called, it is more likely to be a white officer interfacing with a black resident (or potential criminal). When an officer that doesn't identify with a civilian in that time of interaction, bad things can happen like what happened to Alton Sterling. The call came in about a man in front of a store selling CDs with a gun on him.

Even though Louisiana is an Open Carry State which allows a citizen to carry firearms in public openly, the white officers shot and killed Alton because of it. White officers are more than likely living in white communities and going to the black ones to go to patrol and work. Even if the white officers lived in the black community, he or she may or may not still view the black people in that community a certain way because they have to police them and inadvertently mainly see the criminal behavior they exhibit.

When the community begins to police itself, meaning hiring the people in their neighborhoods to uphold law and order we will be more likely to comply and less liable to escalate a moment of conflict because of lack of commonalities.

Because our officers are from the communities they patrol, they will work to end the violence and crime and uplift the standards of living there and not work to terrorize or abuse the other people in the community.

Our officers will treat the residents with respect, kindness and decency while protecting and serving them on the streets from danger and crime. Of course this isn't to say that all white police officers who patrol black communities are racist, just showcasing the importance of self-regulation.

We must realize that police officers can be just as affected, if not more affected by the social ills and crime that we face in the community. It takes a certain level of bravery, humility, and sacrifice to meet these problems head on and many don't realize that police officers are human just like the people they protect and serve.

How many dead bodies could you stomach seeing and smelling every day? How good are you at diffusing situations of conflict without becoming violent? Could you take another person's life if it came down to it and still live with yourself after? These are scenarios that police officers are faced with daily, and we must know if these recruits can handle them properly.

Investing three hundred million dollars ($300,000,000) in each police department we build will allow us the funding to build police stations, pay for uniforms, train officers, pay for police cars and trucks, pay salaries and benefits for the officers, etc. A fully funded police department will help keep our communities together, ultimately doing away with the tension and turmoil Black Americans have with the police.

More of our friends and families will become police officers. The public will be able to trust their police department which will make it easier for them to cooperate when interacting with one another. Children will aspire to be police officers again.

When you combine the solutions of job creation and proper policing, you get a drastic drop in criminal activity. It will no longer be acceptable or attractive to commit crime because of the vast amount of opportunity in any given community. Because of this, the daring who will still commit crimes will be brought to justice in a productive, proactive way. Crime should not be glorified in any shape or form because it allows people to think the behavior is acceptable, which we know is not. We must hold ourselves and each other accountable for the things we do in the community, and it must be understood that we do not condone criminal activity.

Do I believe that the crime in the black community or elsewhere will be completely gone because of this? No, but I do believe that most people are inherently good which is why when criminal activity is glorified, it is made to seem like a good thing. You rarely hear or see individuals who commit crime speak on how bad crime is, but still participate in it. Shooting your neighbor must be made into a good thing or else the shootings wouldn't happen as much.

To a criminal, crime is right way of life and it is up to the people that know better to stop enabling this kind of behavior. It is illogical and hypocritical to glorify or justify crime and then protest when a crime is committed against you or your loved ones. In reverse, it is very logical to glorify civil togetherness and be happy when it is done to you and your loved ones. I predict that the crime rates will be at least cut in half when we build our communities back up, with projections of a seventy-five to eighty-five percent (75%-85%) drop in the long term.

Building local fire departments is another institution that not only creates jobs, but saves lives. Per the National Fire Protection Agency (NFPA), there were over one million (1,298,000) reported fires in the United States, over three thousand (3,275) deaths, almost sixteen thousand (15,775) injuries and a total of over eleven billion dollars ($11,600,000,000) in damages in 2014. Our fire departments will be able to assist in decreasing those numbers and keeping our communities safe.

Just like building our police departments we must research and learn the rules and regulations of the industry to find out how to manifest these ideas into reality. For instance, in Philadelphia, fire departments are regulated through the Philadelphia Fire Code which details all the requirements, inspections, guidelines and laws that govern the Fire Department in the city. It is likely to be available to other cities in the same fashion. Filling out the necessary paperwork, purchasing the necessary insurances and passing the necessary inspections is key to starting any institution, and we must apply the same steps with our emergency departments.

Investing two hundred million dollars ($200,000,000) each fire department will provide us the necessary funding to establish firehouses, equipment, fire trucks and other emergency vehicles, salary for firefighters and first responders and compensation for volunteers, etc. The Fire Department budget matches the budget of major cities like Detroit which spent almost one hundred and fifty million dollars ($142,525,305) in 2015-2016 on their Fire Department.

This initiative includes building our own Emergency Medical Services (EMS) as well. Having teams of Emergency Medical Technicians (EMTs), Paramedics and ambulances in the community will increase the amount of lives saved and help decrease the number of people living with curable diseases. Black American EMS providers, like the Fire Departments, will be headquartered centrally in the community, sometimes within the firehouses to quicken the response time to the scene of an emergency.

Because the EMS is rooted in providing immediate good health restoration to the community, having an EMS staff that practices good health habits will show the ones in need a healthier alternative to certain things that pertain to their ailment. For instance, a call comes in about a potential heart attack in progress. The EMTs and Paramedics arrives quickly, rescues the patient and then educates and assists them in things that can prevent another heart attack.

Since the EMTs and Paramedics are the ones who saved that person's life, their advice will have a higher probability of being accepted and applied to their lives. According to the Fire Brigades Union in the United Kingdom, their Firefighters saved over thirty-eight thousand (38,325) lives from fires and other emergencies like road accidents, floods or chemical spills in 2014.

Based on the numbers of each population alone we can estimate that American firefighters save approximately twenty percent more lives at almost two million (1,899,000) people. This would make sense given that there are nearly one million one hundred thousand firefighters (1,100,000) in the United States.

When the Social Service section is fulfilled and completed we will have solidified safe, united, sustainable and thriving communities throughout the country. Black Americans have the resources to solve whatever problems they're faced with entirely. The elevation of social status amongst ourselves will then translate to non-black Americans communities, enhancing the dynamics of race relations in this country.

Section 11: Politics

Black Americans must become more instrumental in their local governments to provoke change on a legislative level. Grooming, vetting, funding, and voting for people to represent us in local administration is critical to our overall empowerment. Black Americans need a political party first and foremost.

Creating a Third Political Party will establish a regulatory state of independence for Black Americans because we will have control over who and what we elect to represent us. For the sake of this book, we will call it the Black American Political Party. The Libertarian Party is the largest third political party with a little over four hundred thousand (411,250) registered members.

Because most Black American share common political goals in this country, if we acquired just ten percent (10%) of our population at approximately four million three hundred thousand registered voters and members (4,300,000), the BAPP can become major in this country, particularly on the local level.

Because of the 2016 election season, Americans are all more politically aware than any other time in this country. Debates about whose Presidential candidate is better, whether they will fulfill their promises to the people, or if the system is rigged altogether. Even though we pay a great deal of attention to the National elections, not enough is given to the local elections. A good friend of mine and Harvard student studying Quantitative Analysis, Damon Kirk explains the importance of local elections in the black community.

"The average American waits every four years to express their complaints with their community and living standards. Not realizing the local elections are the deciding factor in their biggest complaints. For example; police interactions with Black Males (Attorney General,

election every four years), Discriminatory Laws (State Congress, elections every two years), School Funding and Resources (Local City Council, election every two to four years), and finally accessible recreational activities (City Manager & County Commissioner).

Once you realize how the power is delegated, you'll see the President himself is hardly bothered by direct involvement in our inner cities. I hazard an example; you'd never go to your company's owner to fix something that happens in your particular store."

The Black American Political Party will groom, fund and vote for their own State Senators, State Representatives/Assembly Persons, Mayors, Governors, District Attorney, Board Commissioners, Executives, Auditors, Engineers, Treasurers, Prosecutors, Coroners, Judges, Recorders, Law Directors, City/Town Council Executives, Councilmen/Aldermen, School Board Members, etc. Appointing and electing people from our community into these offices gives us a political leg to stand on in this country.

It doesn't take a Political Scientist to figure out that Black Americans are deeply affected by the current political system they live in. Politicians rarely speak on issues dealing with Black Americans even when they are officials in predominantly black cities. Then you may have a politician or two take the floor on the issues, but never do much of anything about it. A big reason for this is because we are not vetting these officials before we cast our votes.

I had a chance to interview a young man by the name of Jewell Jones, the youngest councilman in Inkster, Michigan at twenty years old. In the interview Councilman Jones spoke to me about creating and renovating the local parks, fixing the problems pertaining to their schools shutting down and lack of transportation for the students, and making the streets safer for the people in Inkster. The interview left me inspired, showing me that the youth coming up are not accepting the living conditions they're growing up in.

We need to encourage more of our community to get involved in their local politics and one of the greatest ways is creating a party that resonates with the people. The truth of the matter is, the two parties that we are taught to support are two sides of the same coin. Democrats and Republicans debate back and forth about ideals, but it always seems like the country is either remaining stagnant or getting worse.

Black Americans participate in this largely because they have the right to and are seeking some change through a system that was taught brings them, but to no avail when it comes to the issues directly pertaining to them. This is where the Black American Political Party comes into play. The BAPP will cater to the problems and pursue viable solutions for them that work in the best interest of the party as a collective.

Our elected legislators will be able to draft laws that cater to the livelihoods of the people and pass them in the community. Legislation that gives people access to proper healthcare, jobs, homes and other resources. Having our own political party encourages young men and women to become registered voters, garnering more support for our elected officials. The more people that get involved, the more change we can implement.

Community participation is just as important as the elected officials themselves. The community must research the people that are running their city and state. The lack of attendance in local government meetings are a big reason why Black Americans find themselves reacting to policy rather than being proactive in the political process. The community must exercise their rights in their local government to demand proper representation.

If an official isn't doing what they proposed in their campaign then, the community can come together and vote that official out (impeach) and replace them with someone better suited for that position. We do not have to tolerate officials who aren't doing their job and it is our Constitutional right as American citizens to seek and exercise governmental action.

A big factor that goes into getting people elected is of course funding. Candidates must have the necessary capital to be able to run a solid campaign and solve issues. For instance, if a man or woman from the BAPP wanted to run for State Senator, the average price of a winning six-year term seat is about ten and a half million dollars ($10,476,451). The average cost for a seat in House of Representatives is about two million dollars ($1,689,580).

As we have already established in this book, Black Americans can afford to support and fund these campaigns. By maintaining a Political budget of ten billion dollars ($10,000,000,000), we will always have the resources ready to back our candidates and officials throughout the duration of their careers. When we have a community that is actively participating in their local government as well as well funding officials, we will see an exponential change in our social, economic and political status in this country.

Because we know we can afford to fund seats at the House and the Senate, we can also afford to do the same throughout the local level. In the interview with Councilman Jones, he told me the name of the game is "Dollars & Doors," being able to reach as many people possible and garnering financial support from them. Like Jones, we must groom our officials and educate them on their position and what they can do with it.

Aspiring Senators will be educated on what it means to be one, likewise for the Executives, Aldermen, Treasurers, etc. and build a plan for what they are going to do if elected into office. This way the community is involved throughout the entire process and knows who and what they're voting for. Black Americans will no longer be in the dark about how their government works and use that knowledge to make our communities a better place to live in.

Black judges will preside over court cases and implement smarter sentencing practices for offenders. From 1970 to 2005, American incarceration rates rose over seven hundred percent (700%). One in fifteen Black American men are incarcerated in this country, making up sixty percent (60%) of all prisons and jails. These numbers mirror in relation to black women as well. Having black judges, lawyers, attorneys and prosecutors will decrease these numbers which will allow for more productive men and women in the community.

The more people able to work in the Black American economy, the larger it becomes. The fewer people we have clogging our jails and prisons, the more people we must employ, educate and empower. Reuniting families torn by a harsh judicial system is just one of the many things Black

Americans can do when we get involved in our local and state politics. Black Americans having a larger presence in the American political arena gives the opportunity to finally do away with a lot of the misfortune that's been incurred in the community.

Wealth Building:

Where Do We Start?

I'm confident that after reading all these economic possibilities you are inspired to know how to start. *"Yes, these things sound fantastic in theory, but how can Black Americans transform this into reality?"* you're probably thinking to yourself. The answer lies within your money managing skills. Black Americans must become more disciplined with their money, cutting back from certain behaviors and relocating our funds into better vehicles for financial growth.

Taking your funds out of the major banks you're used to and putting them in black owned financial institutions will provide an economic base for Black America to work from. I encourage all those willing to open a bank account with OneUnited Bank and financial institutions like it.

The accumulation of black wealth in black financial institutions gives us the ability to start building all the industries mentioned in this book. This is a very crucial step for Black Americans because the longer we keep our money in these major banks, the longer they can fund projects across the globe that empowers their interests with our dollars.

Once we have our funds placed in black financial institutions, we must look at our personal budgets and plan per our income levels. No longer can Black Americans pride themselves on living beyond their means only to end up in crushing bad debt in the long run for the sake of present luxuries. Black Americans must practice proper budgeting to accumulate wealth. Budgeting is not the daunting task that many perceive it to be, it is an enjoyable practice once you get the hang of it.

First, you want to take record all the money you will make in a 30-day period. Then you want to subtract all your bills and direct financial responsibilities from that sum of money. The money that is leftover is what many refer to as "disposable income." Typically, your disposable income is made up of luxuries like clothes, dining, entertainment, alcohol and tobacco, electronic devices, furniture and gifts, vehicles, etc. The idea of budgeting your disposable income is two-fold.

On the one hand, Black Americans must cut back on their irresponsible consumption of nonessential items, freeing up funds to save or invest; and on the other hand they must also use it to patronize black businesses in their community and elsewhere. These two aspects are vital and are at the heart of our economic development.

A reality that I've noticed over the course of my research for this book is the psychology behind being a consumer in America. What people may not know is that when it comes to advertising, the focus isn't really on the product, but the lifestyle the product exudes when you buy it. Most consumers are buying into the desired concept of reality that's being associated with the product just as much, if not more than the actual product itself.

For instance, NIKE will advertise how determined, focused, goal oriented, athletic and vigorous a person who wears their clothing and apparel is. The advertisement speaks little of the benefits and features of the product because they want you to see yourself in the spokesperson of their company.

People want to be more like the spokesperson and what they represent, so to feel like they can achieve that they purchase the product, subconsciously believing that it will help them attain those goals. The most famous example of this would be the 1989 NIKE Air Jordan "It's Gotta be the Shoes" campaign. In the commercial, director Spike Lee speculated that all of Jordan's skill on the court could be attributed to his sneakers (that you should purchase).

People buy things that represent a class or caliber of person they want to identify with, and more times than not it leaves them broke, in debt and unhappy. Living within your means is a fundamental principle in maintaining your budget, and I highly suggest` people look at the things they own that is costing them money in comparison to the things they own that makes them money.

Whether it be a car with payments that are too high, a habit or vice that cuts into your budget, subscriptions and memberships to service providers with bills that add up, etc. These things hurt your bottom line at the end of the month or year and should be fixed as soon as possible. The goal is to spend money to make more money.

Section 12:

Housing Budget

Per the Bureau of Labor Statistics, the median income for black families in America is a little over thirty-six thousand dollars ($36,149) a year. The average rent in America is about one thousand dollars ($1,000) a month. The average mortgage is similar at one thousand and sixty-one dollars ($1,061) a month, and the average property tax is $177. The average electricity bill is one hundred and sixteen dollars ($116). The average water bill is between twenty-five ($25) and seventy dollars ($70). The average gas bill is eighty dollars ($80).

Of course, these numbers fluctuate depending on where you live, the size of your home and family, salary, etc. but it is just to serve as an example for the average American home. In this example, the average black family (2 adults and child) spends twelve thousand dollars ($12,000) a year on rent or almost fifteen thousand dollars ($14,856) on their mortgage and property tax.

Nearly fourteen hundred dollars ($1,392) a year on their electricity, a little under six hundred dollars ($570) a year on their water bill and almost one thousand dollars ($960) on their gas bill. This comes to a total between almost fifteen thousand dollars ($14,922) to about eighteen thousand dollars ($17,778) for home expenses in a year.

For the sake of cutting back on the Housing budget, I suggest Black American families combine incomes per household by adding more people wherever possible. Having more people in the house that are bringing in income allows for easier budgeting, saving and investing for everyone in the house. This equally distributes the financial responsibilities between the earners of the household which takes the stress off any given individual.

So instead of just two people splitting the bills down the middle, adding one or more people to the household frees up more money to be saved and invested for every income earner in the house. Earners in the home will come up with financial plans and execute them with the ultimate goal of being entirely bad debt free and financially independent.

An important lesson that I learned from my studies is that a household should be run like a financial institution and a family should be run like a business. Below the surface of the unconditional love and care that comes with family building lies the foundation of economic stability that allows the family to thrive.

A house is meant to facilitate assets and possessions of all values, including the family. Conceptualizing our homes and relatives in this way will help promote actions that result in higher yields of wealth and financial literacy overall.

When decisions are made with an emphasis on economics and real affordability, the family benefits in many ways. Household members will be more financially literate. Accumulated debt and the risk of any further bad debt accumulation will be lowered. Stress levels due to economic disparities decrease which then strengthens the bond between families and household members. This emphasis gives Black American families a whole new outlook on the way they manage their money.

Black Americans have the power to practice these methods of combining households until they are financially stable as an individual or as a family unit. On a single level, once a person has accumulated, saved, and invested enough wealth to move on and start their own household they are more likely to repeat the behaviors they exhibited in the previous home. As a family unit, members of the household have done the same accumulating, saving and investing coupled with the power of numbers resulting in a higher level of financial standing in society.

This means the children in these households are afforded tools that would otherwise be unavailable to them due to low income factors. This opens them up to an entire world of possibilities that they can now explore, discover and build upon. There will be little to no limitations for them. This way of living reaffirms the notion that *"it takes a village..."* and uses it in modern times to ensure the future of a nation.

Black Americans speaking with friends and family members to cohabitate with one another can serve as an excellent way to save and build wealth. Whoever has the most affordable or best conditions of life for economic sustainability invites people they trust to build wealth together by sharing the responsibility of bills, debt consolidation, and money management as a household unit.

Because Housing is the largest yearly expenditure for Black Americans reaching almost half at forty-five and a half percent (45.5%), it stands to reason that they work this budget out for the greater good of our people. Understanding that a large number of Black Americans rent homes, combining incomes and keeping housing costs low is a very critical tactic to economic empowerment.

Per Jarim Person Lynn of Brass Knuckle Finance University, a business dedicated to providing resources for people to empower themselves economically states that people should keep their rent below twenty-five percent (25%) of their gross monthly income when working to get out of debt.

Even though these things can be done as a family unit, they can also be done on an individual level as well. Single persons can implement some of these practices of cutting back to save on their housing expenses. Decreasing the overall housing expenditure in Black America will free up more funds to put in our saving accounts and investment portfolios.

As I stated in the Housing section of the book, owning and controlling homes and renting and leasing them out to the residents in the community is a very lucrative business venture. Property ownership and control in Black America is imperative because it gives the ability to manage the homes, businesses and buildings in any given black community.

Changing the economic practices of the housing industry in Black America to a more affordable and sustainable condition will cut back on the biggest expense we have which will result in more money available to build wealth in other areas. I recently stumbled upon a young man by the name of Jay Morrison. Jay is a Real Estate Investor from Somerville, New Jersey that has made major headway in the industry in the last ten years. While I was tweeting, I found a video of his on YouTube titled *"How to Build Black Wealth"* where he briefly describes the ability to start making passive income by owning and renting out real estate. The scenario he describes is as follows: A single family acquires a Multi-Family home (between 2-4 units) and rents out the remaining units to friends, family and/or neighbors.

In doing this the family is paying down their mortgage while making passive income from the units they're renting out. The great thing about this investment strategy is that it takes little to no money to start because of the FHA government loan where, if your credit permits, you can purchase the home with just three and half percent (3.5%) down payment. Less than perfect credit would usually permit up to ten percent (10%).

Another real estate avenue that I learned about is Creative Finance Investing. In a nutshell, creative finance investing is when you play the middle man between home sellers and buyers who cannot connect, and collect residual and passive income off the deal. Home sellers and buyers use this method for several reasons, a part of your job will be to find out why. Lease option deals are great for beginners in real estate investing because even though you are profiting from the deal, you do not own the property, have the least amount of responsibility and it takes little to no money to start.

A quick example of a good lease option deal would be a seller wanting two hundred thousand dollars ($200,000) for their home, a two thousand dollar ($2,000) down payment and twelve hundred dollars ($1,200) a month for rent. You would then write up a contract agreeing to the terms you and the seller came to (the most relevant being the term for you to be able to "assign" the property to a new tenant buyer) and then market the home yourself to find a new buyer.

You would then ask for two hundred and twenty thousand dollars ($220,000) for the home, a ten thousand dollar ($10,000) down payment, and fourteen hundred dollars ($1,400) a month for rent. After you find a new buyer that agrees to those terms in contract, you pay the seller their asking prices and keep the rest as profit.

In total, you would now have eight thousand dollars ($8,000) profit from the down payment, two hundred dollars ($200) coming in monthly ($2,400 a year), and twelve thousand dollars ($12,000) on the backend of the deal for the sales price. A total of twenty-two thousand and four hundred dollars ($22,400) in one year by simply connecting buyers and sellers. And that was just one deal, imagine doing one of every month.

The amazing thing about these deals are that you don't have to pay the seller until the new buyer pays you, meaning you do not necessarily need money to make money in real estate. Of course, the more money you do use, the easier the process will be. I encourage my readers to take advantage of opportunities like these by educating yourselves and executing it when you are ready.

Think of what you would do if you had an extra few thousand dollars added to your gross monthly and yearly income. You could go on vacation, start or invest in a business or new hobby, purchase assets through your business, enroll for classes, set up a college fund for yourself or your children, maybe even begin a retirement fund. These things will become a reality once Black Americans intelligently work together to reduce the amount of money being spent on the Housing expenditures every month and year. Financial independence is at the nucleus of everything in this book.

This type of budgeting and planning keeps people from being slaves to their own homes and bills. Instead of being past due on these financial obligations people will have the capital to pay them off in an "on-timely" fashion. Now when you come home from school or work, the stress of having a utility shut off because of lack of payment will be far less likely in the black community. Residents can happily afford to own their possessions and not have it repossessed because of nonpayment. This changes the mindset of people to being creditors and not debtors. This promotes ownership, control, financial accountability and civil togetherness in the homes of Black America.

Collaborating in pursuit of a common goal is very necessary for a disunited disenfranchised people. Black Americans will be metaphorically killing two birds with one stone in this budgeting plan. We will be coming together and trusting one another, solving the disunity factor and then we will be doing it in the name of saving and investing money which solves the disenfranchised aspect of Black America. This is better than getting external aid because this keeps the control of the process inside Black America and nowhere else.

Section 13:

Food Budget

When it comes to food, it would be intelligent for people not to buy unhealthy processed foods and meats to save money. This includes Fast Food and chain restaurants. This not only saves money, but it also adds to your overall health in the short and long term.

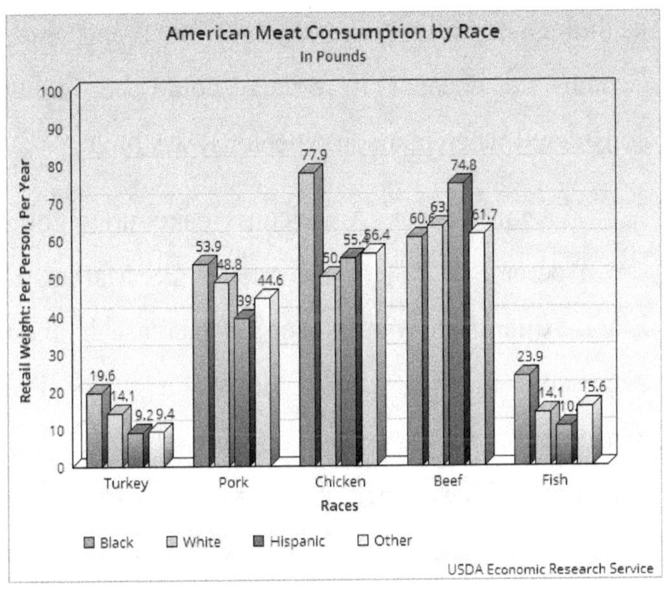

Graphed above is the amount of meat consumed per pound per year by race in America. According to the USDA, Black Americans consume the most meat in the country. Black households consume almost twenty pounds (19.6) of Turkey, nearly fifty-four pounds (53.9) of Pork, almost twenty-four pounds (23.9) of Fish, approximately seventy-eight pounds (77.9) of Chicken and a little under sixty-one pounds (60.6) of Beef every year. Cutting back on meat and replacing them with healthier alternatives like legumes, nuts, and seeds (which are cheaper in price) should be highly considered when managing personal wealth.

Again, Black Americans make up eighty-seven percent (87%) of the overall US Market. If Black Americans want to see an increase in their disposable income, cutting down on their meat consumption should be one of the first things they do. Think of how much money you spend on meat and add it back to your disposable income and you'll see how much you will ultimately save.

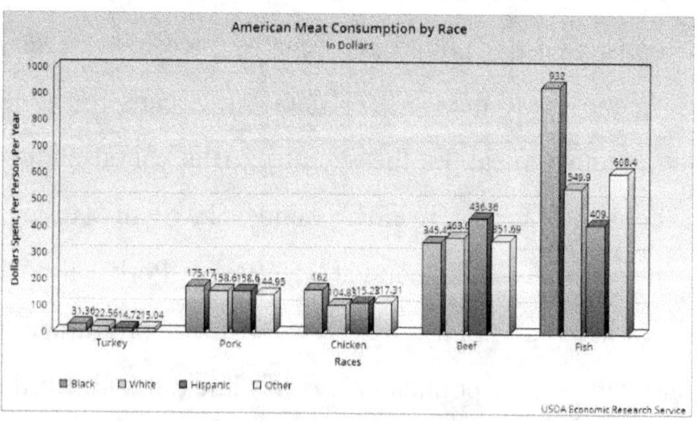

Graphed above is the meat consumption from the previous chart, translated to how much people spend on meat in a year. Black American households spend thirty-one dollars ($31.36) on Turkey, one hundred and seventy-five dollars ($175.17) on Pork, nine hundred and thirty-two dollars ($932) on Fish and Seafood, one hundred and sixty-two dollars ($162) on Chicken and three hundred and forty-five dollars ($345) on Beef every year.

As we can see, a vegetarian/vegan lifestyle saves hundreds, if not thousands of dollars in a year and I encourage people to make the change, not just for economic prosperity, but also for their health benefit.

Even if you do not decide to change your diet, please still reduce your meat consumption according to how much money you would like to save. When we cut meat from our diets, the average amount of money spent on groceries decreases dramatically, leaving more disposable income that can be saved and invested.

For this, try buying only fruits, vegetables, nuts, grains, seeds, legumes, herbs, spices and roots for your food instead of eating processed foods and meats and dining out. The average family of four spends about two hundred dollars ($203) a week on groceries per the USDA Food Plan of 2016, or up to eight hundred dollars ($812) or more a month, depending on the household.

In fact, Americans for the first time ever spent more money on dining out than eating at home. I estimate much of these grocery bills are made up of processed foods, dairy, and meat products because those items cost more versus the price of fresh produce.

Another viable solution and ultimately the best option is starting your own garden or farm and growing your own food. Think of growing your own food as an investment in your grocery bill. The National Gardening Association reports ***"A well-maintained food garden can yield an estimated ½ pound of produce per square foot of garden area***

over the course of the growing season. At in-season market prices, this produce is worth $2.00 per pound. The average 600-square-foot food garden can produce an estimated 300 pounds of fresh produce worth $600 and a return of $530 based on an average investment of $70.”.

If you invested one hundred ($100) to five hundred dollars ($500) in your home garden, you could ultimately feed yourself and your family for the entire year, cutting up to seventy-five percent (75%) of your grocery budget. Because most people can grow food three seasons out of the year, it allows for people to maintain and plan your food supply for the winter months.

At the end of the day, Black Americans stand to profit the most when reorganizing our food budgets. Starting gardens in the yards, windows and lots of homes will save so much money in the short and long term. What I also know is that lifestyle changes such as these take commitment and discipline to make it last for any amount of time.

We must combat the urge to buy foods when we know it's not in our budgets (or healthy for us). We must learn to say no to dining out or other luxuries when we cannot afford it. These things take time, willpower and with determination will be done.

Eating right is essential to any progress looking to be made by a nation. As previously stated, if we do not have our health we have nothing. All the money in the world won't matter if people are not physically and mentally healthy to utilize it. A Black American diet change is extremely crucial today, and I encourage everyone reading to make that adjustment.

Black Americans can cut their grocery bill in at least half when they cut meat out their diets, even more, if they cut out dairy products. Reconfigure your dollars to patronize black owned restaurants and food service providers. Pay attention to how much money you spend on food and plan your budget accordingly to save and gain as much money as possible.

Section 14:

Clothing Budget

Black Americans must also look at their clothing budget and make changes accordingly. Per the Bureau of Labor Statistics (BLS), Black Americans spend thirty percent (30%) of their disposable income on things like entertainment, clothing, insurances and other expenses outside of Housing and Transportation.

So, that means if you made the average black income of thirty-six thousand dollars ($36,149) a year, you spent almost eleven thousand dollars ($10,844.69) of your income on these things. That is a massive amount of consuming, and we must cut back and educate ourselves on the importance of gaining wealth through those expenses (instead of losing money) to ensure financial independence.

When it comes to clothing, Black Americans can afford to cut back, especially when most of the brands they financially support is not black owned. Clothing brands like NIKE, Ralph Lauren and H&M, etc. are some of the most commonly worn brands in the black community. Black Americans must look at how much money they spend on clothing for a change to take place.

Look at your dresser drawers and closets, do you honestly need to buy more clothing? And if you do, are the brands you're ready to shop with black owned? If you're like most people, you don't NEED any more clothes; you WANT more which isn't necessarily a bad thing.

Per Experian Information Solutions, Inc. ***"African Americans are 78% more likely than average to say they no longer wear clothes they wore a year ago because they have gone out of style."***. This sentiment means that Black Americans are continuously and perpetually buying more and more clothing even though they don't necessarily have to. Not only that, but most American blacks are discarding old clothing because they deem them "out of style." Over time this creates a vicious habit of frivolously spending money on nonessential items, which then ultimately hurts your personal wealth.

I suggest Black Americans stop patronizing these major brands as much, save their funds and then patronize black owned clothing brands and fashion designers instead. What this does is keep Black American dollars in Black America longer. The money you save from not spending so much can be used to invest in businesses or ideas that can potentially create more wealth. Then when you do go clothes shopping, the black businesses you patronize can grow and expand.

As I stated in the Finance section, investing in the black companies you frequently patronize is a better way for you to spend money because the better the company does, the better your portfolio looks. Investing in the black owned clothing brands in this case virtually ensures more income for the shopper and the brand at the same time.

As a simplified example, instead of just spending six hundred dollars with a brand (not getting any money in return), you can invest that money and negotiate a return on investment with that brand. An average return on investment for small business is between 25-50 percent (25-50%) annually. Meaning you would get between one hundred and fifty ($150) and three hundred dollars ($300) back every year, more if you make additional monthly contributions throughout those twelve months.

Let's say the manufacturing costs to make a full run of t-shirts of every size from a Small up to an XX-Large is ten dollars ($10) per shirt. This means the six-hundred-dollar investment pays for the manufacturing of twelve shirts of each size. If the clothing brand sells the shirts for twenty-five dollars ($25) each they stand to make up to fifteen hundred dollars ($1,500) from the shirts in total.

The clothing brand is now able to pay another six hundred dollars ($600) from their revenue and restock their order (40%), give a return on investment in the amount of seven hundred and fifty dollars ($750) (50%), and take in profits of one hundred and fifty dollars ($150) or ten percent (10%).

Even though the return of investment is fifty percent (50%) of the clothing brand's revenue, it is only a twenty-five percent (25%) return on the investment. The clothing brand now has the capital to continue to make shirts and bring in further profits while the investor also benefits from the endeavor. The investor and the clothing brand may choose to keep working together over the course of time or let it be a onetime transaction.

Of course, in the application, there will be other negotiated variables that the brand and the investor will come to terms with, this just serves as a general example for the sake of this book.

The average black household spends one thousand dollars ($1,000) on Apparel and Services every year. This may not seem like a lot of money, but the average black household size is just two adults and a child. Also, this is based on the mean of all black families of all financial standings in the United States. When we add more people and/or raise the income of the household, consumption of clothing increases.

When Black Americans spend their clothing budget exclusively or predominantly with black owned clothing brands, those brands can build storefronts, hire employees and compete in the fashion markets nationally and even globally.

There is an abundance of black owned clothing brands that are waiting to serve the people and it's time those designers get our dollars over the household names we are used to. Now is the time to make these brands the new household names.

Overall, this method of cutting back and relocating funds can be applied to almost every aspect of the Black American Budget to make sure our money circulates and accumulates in the community first and foremost. We must work with the businesses and methods we have so we can use that wealth to create even more firms that offer the other goods and services we need. It all depends on how much money we spend with them on a regular basis.

It must become second nature for Black Americans to look at their purchases as investments. If whatever you are buying isn't helping your livelihood in any way, then it should not be high on the priority list. When you buy food, it should add to your health. When you consume entertainment, it should add to your artistry. When you buy your transportation, it should add to your independence and freedom, not take away from it.

This point of view allows people to see how passive income and generational wealth is created.

Because you are trying to have the things you buy multiply in benefits, frivolous spending won't be as attractive anymore.

It'll become easy to pass on the one dollar McDonald's burger because you'll know the cost of that burger multiples when you factor the cost to manufacture it and the cost on your health. It will be easier for you to invest in a higher quality restaurant experience, buy the ingredients to make yourself, or grow your own food.

Instead of buying garments made with slave labor from major retailers, we will invest in local clothing brands to make our clothing. This is especially important because of how frequently Black Americans discard old clothing. When we invest in clothes that were made for us, we will wear it longer. When customers build a relationship with the brand, they'll hold their products in a higher regard.

It is very easy to discard a $10 shirt that was mass produced in a sweatshop because we know we can always go back and buy another one. When the clothing is made by designers who take pride in their craft, the integrity of the garment increases to the point you must appreciate it more than the average garment.

This crosses over into every industry in this book and beyond. There are millions of people in the black community that offer an array of goods and services to the world; we must find and fund them. Whether it's a plumber, a tutor or a wedding planner, it is crucial to seek out small/local professionals to get the job done. When this becomes a habit for black consumers, we will see a drastic change in the black community.

This type of budgeting keeps debt accumulating expenses low and clothing supply high in the household. There's nothing wrong with being fashionable and trendy. People have the right to wear what they please, but it should not come at the price of being poor at the end of the month.

Socially we must change our mindsets on what clothing means to us in relation to our budgets. I do believe that people should present themselves to the public in the best ways possible, but the definition of "presentable" usually means buying clothes based on the social status that comes with the wearing them. There are plenty of ways to still present yourself in a fashionable way without breaking the bank. One of the biggest avenues is thrift stores, consignment stores and secondhand shops that offer garments at affordable prices. Some may turn their noses up at the thought of this, but it has been proven to save money.

Most thrift and secondhand stores offer goods (including clothing) that reach well over sixty percent (60%) off their original retail prices, a lot of which are from "presentable" brands. With slight alterations to these garments and a deep cleaning, we will have successfully saved tremendous amounts of money by shopping this way.

Combining the methods of consumption reduction, thrifting, shopping small and locally and investing in clothing brands will allow Black Americans to see a significant cut in the clothing budget, a major increase in our personal wealth while still having all the garments we desire, and a thriving fashion industry.

We don't have to sacrifice our fashion sense to be fiscally responsible, but we must sacrifice the behavior of going broke to look rich. Shopping within a clothing budget and not deviating from it will allow Black Americans to be just as fashionable while still building wealth.

Section 15:

Getting Out of Debt

Another major problem that the method of saving helps solve is the accumulation of bad debt. You may be wondering why I consistently have been distinguishing debt by calling it "bad," insinuating that there is good debt.

While vending at a Yoga Festival in rural Pennsylvania with my wife, I was given a book for free from a group of women that was set up just a few feet away from our station. The book was *"Rich Dad's Guide to Investing: What the Rich Invest In, That the Poor and Middle Class Do Not!"* This book opened my eyes to a different world of financial literacy that I personally never knew existed. In the book author Robert T. Kiyosaki detailed the difference between good and bad debt.

"As a general rule, good debt, good expenses, and good losses all generate additional cash flow for you. For instance, debt taken to acquire a rental property, which has a positive cash flow each month, would be good debt."

There is a such thing as good debt, and people should take advantage of it once they become more financially literate, but what this section is about is getting out of bad debt. Let's say you like your job but are swamped in debt; you can dedicate ten to twenty percent (10-20%) of your income to paying off whatever debt you may have incurred, gradually chipping away at it until it's settled. Being bad debt free should be a top priority.

Reconciling bad debt will be one of the most important things Black Americans will do with their money. Setting up a plan to proactively pay off debt takes proper budgeting and spending for someone to make any financial progress.

A report from the research and policy think tank Demos and the NAACP titled *"The Challenge of Credit Card Debt for the African American Middle Class"* states that forty-two percent (42%) of Black American households use credit cards to pay for basic living expenses like rent, mortgage payments, groceries, utilities, or insurance because they do not have enough money in their checking or savings accounts. This can be fixed.

As we can see our credit card purchases surround most of the same things we have already discussed in this book, the essentials. When we lower the cost of housing, food, bills, and clothing we will see how much easier it is to reduce debt. This freed up money will go directly to paying off our credit cards and other forms of bad debt. In this endeavor, please do not underestimate the power of accumulation of small purchases.

Purchases like a daily cup of coffee accumulate over time. If your daily cup of coffee costs three dollars ($3), in a year you have spent almost eight hundred dollars ($780), and that's only counting workdays. If we factor in all days of the year, the figure reaches over one thousand dollars ($1,095). This is only accounting for one cup of coffee; Americans drink an average of three cups of coffee per day.

Expenses like these happen often and can go undetected when budgeting. That money could have been used to pay off a bill or a bad debt that's hurting your bottom line. It may seem small during a transaction, but as we can see it quickly adds up. Paying attention to, cutting back and then ultimately profiting from these little purchases will help us get out of bad debt.

An inconvenient truth about getting out of bad debt is the realization that people truly cannot afford some of the things they have and freeing themselves of these additional responsibilities will be a major factor. This isn't to say that people will never be able to afford them, but for the sake of getting out of bad debt, these things must take the backseat to more immediate obligated expenses. If you're in perpetual bad debt, you'll never be able to accumulate wealth because it only takes away money, never adds.

Living within your means does not say that you must live miserable unfulfilling lives, it's quite the opposite. Ninety percent (90%) of American millionaire households say they are satisfied with their lives living in homes that cost three hundred thousand dollars ($300,000) or less.

I understand that happiness in America has long been equated to the acquisition of material goods. This isn't a bad thing, but when people sacrifice their well-being and peace of mind in the pursuit of these material goods they will never be satisfied no matter how many of these things they acquire. Our minds and bodies won't allow it.

Concepts like "retail therapy" are surrounded around healing ourselves through consumption. Per a survey done by the Huffington

Post, one in three stressed Americans used retail therapy to deal with anxiety. Meaning that it wasn't until these people bought something that they could feel better about themselves.

This mentality and behavior manifests itself in other aspects of our lives as well. The survey also showed that these same people were eighty-six percent (86%) more likely to consume food to alleviate stress, seventy-six percent (76%) are more liable to stress over their weight, and forty-six percent (46%) are more liable to exercise to deal with stress.

It's easy to see how these things can be a problem for people's budgets, but it also shows how they are conditioned to look outward for consumable goods to heal themselves instead of looking inward. Coping with stress through material means will always end in unhappiness because as cliché as it may sound, happiness comes from within. That new piece of clothing or that snack is only a temporary fix to a deeper-rooted problem, and people owe it to themselves to find out what they are and proactively solve them.

I'm no therapist, but what I do know from my own experiences is that everything starts in the mind. From the smile on our faces to the stress that we feel at school or work, it all began as a thought in the mind.

There are plenty of exercises and behaviors that can be implemented without spending additional amounts of money like yoga, meditation, going for walks, regular workouts, writing a journal, picking up a new productive hobby, volunteering, talking to a friend, even eating certain fruits, vegetables and herbs can improve our state of mind. Finding positive alternatives for bad habits is essential to this type of growth.

This not only saves you money, but it also allows you to heal yourself instead of solely relying on outside materials to feel better. In my journey, I found that if my mind isn't working at full capacity, then neither will my body. If my body isn't working at full capacity, then I can't produce the way I should. And if I can't produce then I am of no use, not even to myself.

We cannot separate our minds from our finances because they work in tandem. In this endeavor of getting out of bad debt, we will see how our mindsets will change to accumulate wealth (knowledge), just like our spending habits and bank accounts. Being able to rely on ourselves for much of our needs will be crucial in this initiative.

Self-sufficiency is a major key to saving money and budgeting. Being able to provide your own essentials is the sure way to never having to struggle again. You will never be hungry when your garden is full. You will never be naked when you know how to sew your own clothes. You will never be homeless when you know how to build a house. You will never be thirsty if you know how to harvest water. You will never be without power when you know how to harness your own energy.

In 2016 and beyond these skills aren't as socially relevant as they once were, but they still serve the same purposes, and people should be able to provide these things for themselves. The largest expenditure for Black Americans is their homes, at over forty percent. This means that we spend the bulk of our money on our homes and most our time at a job to maintain the home.

We've seen creative blurbs about the monotony of the nine to five and most of it is true. Participating in work that isn't fulfilling to what you believe to be your purpose in life can take a significant toll on your wellbeing. People who live life this way are primarily participating in this behavior because of financial obligation. Bills need to be paid, so generating income is a top priority by any means necessary. Therefore, budgeting is of the utmost importance.

Living "check to check" may be a reality now, but it can change once you choose to accumulate your earnings instead of spending it. If possible, save and/or invest ten to twenty percent (10-20%) of your income and let it accumulate over time. This means if you make the average black household income of three thousand dollars ($3,012) a month, you will save between three hundred ($300) and six hundred dollars ($600) which add to thirty-six hundred ($3,600) and seventy-two hundred dollars ($7,200) annually.

This still frees up money to spend on food, clothing, insurances, emergencies, entertainment and other expenses. When you apply this way of saving along with short and long term financial goals, you can plan to quit the cycle of monotony and pursue more fulfilling work. Now you will have a sum of money to fund your dream job or live off while you look for better opportunities.

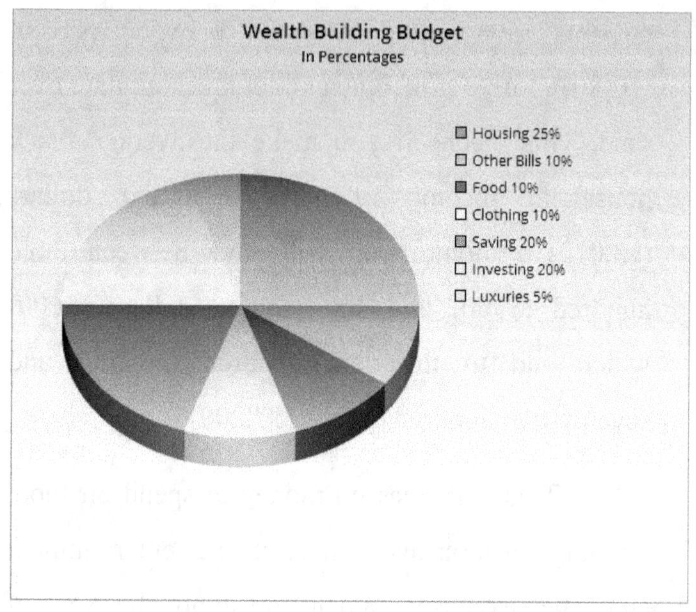

The Wealth Building Budget (charted above) is the ideal budget for Black Americans. Housing costs being twenty-five percent (25%), or lower of your gross monthly income. Other bills like insurances, credit cards, car payments, etc. at ten percent (10%), Food expenses at ten percent (10%), Clothing costs at ten percent (10%) (Seasonal), saving up to twenty percent (20%), investing up to twenty percent (20%) and five percent (5%) for luxuries. This can be customized to fit individual households, adding and/or subtracting in certain categories, but ultimately this is the budget that will get us out of bad debt and accumulating wealth.

Per the Demos/NAACP report ***"79 percent of African American households with a credit card carry credit card debt. With a typical credit card debt burden of $5,784, the average African American household in our survey owes credit card companies as much as 13 percent of their annual income."*** with our Wealth Building Budget in mind, Black Americans can reconcile their credit card debt in a year or two years' time. There's no need to stay in bad debt just to make ends meet. All we must do is change the requirements of the ends and live within or lower than the means.

In *"Meet the Millionaire Next Door"* Stanley & Danko's surveys and studies found that most millionaires spent less money than most people earning lower incomes. Timex is the number one watch brand among millionaires instead of

Breitling or Rolex. Most millionaires never spend more than four hundred dollars ($399) for a suit or outfit. Half of the millionaires surveyed reported they never spend more than one hundred and forty dollars ($140) on a pair of shoes.

If we allow popular culture to control the narrative of the lifestyles of the rich, they would say the complete opposite. Television and the internet show the millionaires that go on massive shopping sprees and elaborate lifestyles even though they are the minority of all millionaires in the United States. The previously stated guise of "happiness through consumption" via pop culture and society hinders the average American's chance of accumulating real wealth in their lifetime.

Everyone is taught that life is short so we must "do it up" before it's all over. In one way, I agree, we should take full advantage of the life that was given to us, but we must still understand that our actions have repercussions and consequences to them in the immediate and distant future. They can be either right or wrong in nature.

The "you only live once" "you can't take it with you when you're gone" mentality has done lots of damage, particularly to the lower income demographics. Innately the poor want to become the wealthy; it's embedded in the mind of the people that they want to live a more affluent lifestyle. From birth, they are taught that rich people buy certain expensive material goods to show their wealth and then later backed up by seemingly wealthy people exhibiting these same behaviors in the media.

So here we are in America where the poor and middle classes pay top dollar to look and live like the rich while the wealthy pay bottom dollar to look and live like the middle class. Most millionaires blend in with Middle Americans, buying subtle homes and staying there their whole lives. Ninety-five percent (95%) of American millionaires are married couples that don't spend much money and when they do, it is to make more money. Their expenses buy assets instead of liabilities. This is the real lifestyle of much of the wealthy. I believe more Black Americans should take note of these behaviors and work to adopt them to create and build more wealth. Buying quality items that last long, eating fresh produce, saving and investing your money and using it to get richer.

Doing this will allow a higher amount of money for luxuries in our budgets. Having accumulated wealth gives people the opportunity to spend money without it the worry of going broke. The average Black American household's Luxury Budget, according to the Wealth Building Budget and average Black American income is one hundred and fifty dollars ($150) a month. If the household income increases so could the luxury budget.

Everybody, especially in the Western world can appreciate indulging in luxury from time to time, but the primary objective is to get to the point of affording these luxuries and not just being able to buy them at the time.

I think it's important for people to know that there is a difference between income and wealth. Income is the money you make every (other) week, month or year via your jobs, businesses, etc. Wealth is the sum of income, assets, and investments you have that accumulates money on its own. So even though someone may earn a lot of money, there's still a chance that person isn't wealthy. Wealth is self-accumulating and managed by hired financial professionals. Meaning that if the fortune is comprised of things that appreciate over time and managed correctly it will automatically increase in value.

Some people have six and seven figure incomes, but no wealth. Largely due to the same reasons people of lower income levels don't have wealth, the lack of financial literacy and massive spending that doesn't end in more money being made. This applies to higher income Black American households especially.

"The annual basket ring (average dollar amount spent per household, per year) for Black households earning between $70,000 and $100,000 per year is $7,358, which is 25% higher than the total Black population. [...] The amount spent on each store visit is also higher for African-Americans who earn $100,000+, with a basket ring per trip that is 40% higher than the total Black population."

- Nielsen Company, 2015

The more income Black American households get, the more they spend on liabilities which will directly reflect the state of little wealth accumulation in the black community. Even though overall revenues are increasing, because Black Americans aren't investing the money in their futures and their communities, the money vanishes almost instantly compared to other groups in the United States.

Wealth is not just about being flashy and flamboyant with your money. Wealth is having your money make more money without having to work for it. How long could you maintain your lifestyle if you lost your job? The answer to that question is the difference between wealth and income.

Credit card debt is a beast in Black America, but luckily for us, we have the ability and the wherewithal to tame it and make it heel to our will. Through discipline and proper execution, credit card debt will be a thing of the past for those who choose to take on these practices. Instead of solely using an external line of credit we will build individual wealth and then bring it together for whatever commercial based endeavors we choose as a collective.

Another form of debt that plagues Black America is student loan debt. The Demos/NAACP report states ***"In 2008, student loan debt affected 15 percent more African American graduates than white graduates. Eighty percent of African American college grads took out some amount of loans in order to attain a higher education,***

compared to 65 percent of whites. In the same year, the average African American senior leaving college with student loans owed $28,692, compared to $24,742 for whites."

Student loan debt is hurting the Black American economy because it seems to be cemented in the minds of many that it will take a lifetime to pay it off. A lot of Black American graduates are entering a workforce that doesn't offer the jobs that their degree promised it would earn them. Most people look at their college education as an investment for their future. Students enroll because the resulting career path of their studies will provide the funds necessary to pay off their loan debt in a reasonable amount of time. What we are seeing is almost the complete opposite.

I believe college gives great life experience and education to people who want to broaden their horizons in many different aspects. I also think people shouldn't put themselves in crippling debt to gain this experience and education. College, like everything else that is considered a "non-essential" for sustaining a living should be something that we embark on when we can afford it. This is where things like college funds, saving and investing come into play. Being able to plan ahead for college, financially puts the student in a better position than one that is using loans to get their education.

Life experience and independent research have shown me that contrary to popular belief college isn't the end all be all for American intelligence and prosperity. Of course, professionals like Doctors and lawyers must attend school to become certified in their fields, but the education is available to them in the form of independent research and smaller and cheaper classes in their surrounding areas.

So even though the aspiring doctor doesn't have the certification of a physician yet, they can use the information they learned in other avenues to help fuel their investment of a college education. If knowledge is the real goal, then we must pursue the lessons and not just the institution it's taught in.

In the pursuit of knowledge, we can save money simultaneously. While we are learning in our respective fields of higher education, we will have a college fund that we will ultimately use to pay our way through college instead of accumulating bad debt.

For students that are pursuing other fields of higher learning that center around entrepreneurship and artistry, I believe the independent research and smaller, cheaper classes are the best options. Because these professions don't necessarily require a doctorate's or a bachelor's degree to practice, aspiring Black American entrepreneurs will build their business endeavors from the ground up. This would mean leading with revenue and profit accumulation rather than bad debt.

So instead of an ambitious businessperson paying one hundred thousand dollars ($100,000) over the course of four years to get a degree in business, they can work to receive investments or grants from black owned institutions or individuals. Twenty-five thousand dollars ($25,000) toward the education of the industry they're pursuing. Seventy thousand dollars ($70,000) to start the business while leaving five thousand dollars ($5,000) as an emergency fund.

This allows the entrepreneurs to make profits while they are getting their education. So, after some time has passed, the self-made entrepreneur now has the money to afford a college education if they choose to enroll. This is a way better approach to higher education and its possibilities than diving head first into a pile of student loan debt.

Now, when we think of the average American college student's spending habits, we think of a medium sized dorm room with stacks of Ramen Noodles and PB&J on top of a microwave. We create images of a student stretching every red cent of their paycheck until the next time they got paid. The struggling college student trope has been a part of pop culture for as long as we can remember. While this may be true for some, overall college students' spending habits, don't show much financial responsibility.

A national survey conducted by EverFi and sponsored by Higher One called *"Money Matters on Campus: Examining Financial Attitudes and Behaviors of Two-Year and Four-Year College Students"* questioned 12,000 students across the United States on their financial literacy and spending habits. Per the survey, the amount of college students that own credit cards has risen thirteen percent (13%) in the years of 2012-2015.

This increase in credit card ownership resulted in an increase of minimum and late bill payments along with higher outstanding balances in those years. Ninety percent (90%) of college students have checking accounts. The report also states that even though there wasn't an increase in students taking out student loans, students are still not paying or even planning to pay off their student loans.

"There were significant decreases over time in nearly all of the responsible fiscal actions that students might take in the next year: following a budget, paying credit card bills on time, reviewing bills for mistakes, saving and investing, paying their entire credit card bill, contacting a credit card bureau, using a debit card rather than credit card for everyday expenses, balancing their checkbooks every month, buying only the things they need and building up an emergency fund."

As we can see, a lot of college students aren't properly preparing themselves financially for the reality of bad debt accumulation through student loans. When we think of all the money that will inevitably be wasted by college students throughout their years in school, we can see how that money should be saved and used to pay off their student loans instead.

Again, we have to stray away from equating having fun or "living life" with frivolous spending, especially in our younger years. These bad spending habits can and more than likely will come back to haunt us as we get older. Once Black American college students start focusing their available funds on saving and investing, they will see a decrease in student loan debt and an increase in Black American college wealth. The money that Black American college students save and invest will allow them to fund their futures in more proactive ways, increasing the chances of them landing the desired occupations of their fields of study.

Current graduates can pay off their student loan debt by applying the same principles we're using for getting out of credit card debt. With a disciplined budget and smarter spending habits, Black American college graduates will reconcile their debts to these institutions.

The more I read about the spending habits of the wealthy, the more I see that the foundation of all wealth building is spending money in places that are necessary to create more wealth and then reducing the cost of liabilities. I can't stress enough how consumption of liabilities is one of the biggest reasons why most people die in debt.

As Americans, we consume so much that it has become a culture. We have national sales holidays like Black Friday that people save and plan for. People trample over and fight one another in the main retailers throughout the country in the late night and early morning hours for items that they could've purchased any other day of the year at roughly the same price.

This is because the lower prices are just incentives for people who are seeking happiness through the consumption of material goods. So even though someone already has a forty-six inch (46") flat screen television in their home, because they're basing their happiness or success levels on the size or definition of their television they will more than likely spend money on Black Friday for a fifty inch (50”) flat screen TV.

Why? Because they may have the funds available to pay for the fifty inch in their account, which translates (to them) to being able to afford it. Then because they believe they can afford it, people feel that they almost have to buy it just to show that they could.

This cycle of habitual spending has been ingrained in people's minds since they were born and because of that, it can be difficult to reverse without the presence of willpower and determination. This isn't to bash consumption altogether, but to get a firm understanding of the difference between assets and liabilities.

Simply put, assets make wealth and liabilities take wealth. Getting out of bad debt as a concept is relatively easy when people break down everything they spend in a month’s and years’ time and then figure out what's costing them money versus what's making them money.

Decreasing consumption of liabilities will also play a role in the replenishing of our environment. Because Black Americans make up eighty seven percent (87%) of the US retail market, when we stop consuming liabilities as much we will also see the brands we were once regular patrons decrease in production for the sake of saving money.

This, of course, alleviates some stress from the environment that is affected by these manufacturing facilities. A reduction in liability consumption will improve our overall health as well. Cutting back on unhealthy meals and snacks and replacing them with much more affordable natural produce will add to our health as well as our bank accounts.

In this instance of getting out of debt and building wealth, less will always be more. Most wealthy people get wealthy by keeping dangerous expenses low and saving and investing high. Gaining wealth and getting rid of bad debt is possible once you do the necessary budgeting, researching and planning for your money. You can never be too mindful of your wealth and how to make it last as long as possible.

Section 16: Boycotting

As Black Americans, we are no stranger to consumer boycotting. In an era where institutionalized racism and discrimination was at an all-time high Black Americans used the empowerment tool of boycotting to send a clear message: *"You don't value our humanity, we won't buy!"* As someone who is fascinated by our buying power in America, I especially gravitated towards a mass of people coming together and not funding an entity that didn't align with their principles.

One of the main boycotts that Black Americans can remember was the boycotting of the public bus company in Montgomery, Alabama. This boycott was America's first major boycotting in history. As a response to the ejecting and jailing of several Black Americans including one Rosa Parks for not giving up their seats for white passengers,

Black Montgomery residents refused to ride the public bus for 381 days.

Starting on December 5, 1955, Black Americans chose to walk to work and school instead of using the racist bus company. Black Taxi companies began to lower their prices to match that of the going bus fare, ten cents. Once city officials caught wind of this they sent out an order to fine any black cab companies that didn't charge at least forty-five cents, the going rate for cab drivers.

In response, Black Americans created private taxi companies that allowed them to charge whatever price they'd like to passengers because it was their personal mode of transport. In essence, Black Americans started the business of private for-profit taxi companies' decades before Uber or Lyft.

In that time the bus company lost so much money that just to stay open and avoid bankruptcy they had to desegregate the buses. Like we see today, Black Americans were seventy-five percent

(75%) of the bus company's passengers. Montgomery at the time was forty-four percent (44%) black, ninety percent (90%) of which rode the bus. This also means they were seventy-five percent of their revenue and profit.

Another aspect of this boycott was the residual boycotting of a lot of white owned stores and shops. When Black Americans would usually ride the bus, they would also be in those areas and spend money with the shops. Since Black Americans centralized their commutes the black dollars stayed in the black community.

This boycott can serve as a microcosm of what this book is about. Black Americans have been fueling the greater economy while not getting anywhere close to a proper return on their patronage for generations. I do not have any negative emotions toward this behavior because I look at it from a business standpoint, not personal.

If someone can proactively discriminate against a group of people while still profiting from them, they would be hard pressed to change their behavior. This is why slave labor is such a prominent tool in mass production. Unethical business practices are widely accepted by the masses, directly or indirectly.

One may not personally think companies using unethical practices are a good thing, but when they purchase goods and services from these firms, the result is no different than a person buying with the sole intent to fuel the practices. The money has no conscience; it goes to the same place regardless of intent.

I stand in the position that Black Americans should scrutinize institutions and businesses based on their ethics. These inhumane actions cannot be tolerated, let alone funded. Another form of unethical labor that American big companies use is what industry heads consider "insourcing" or prison labor.

Prison labor is the forceful employment of prison inmates to manufacture goods at an exponentially lower cost than employing the average citizen or even outsourcing. These companies unethically use the Thirteenth Amendment (which outlaws slavery and involuntary servitude except as a punishment for a crime) to their advantage to "legally" use this form of slavery without being prosecuted themselves.

"On average, prisoners work 8 hours a day, but they have no union representation and make between .23 and $1.15 per hour, over 6 times less than federal minimum wage. These low wages combined with increasing communication and commissary costs mean that inmates are often released from correctional facilities with more debt than they had on their arrival. Meanwhile, big businesses receive tax credits for employing these inmates in excess of millions of dollars a year."

- Kelley Davidson, U.S Uncut, 2015

Seeing that one in fifteen Black American men are incarcerated (compared to one in one hundred and six White American men) we understand that most of this labor is being done by Black American men and women. This is modern day slavery. We have also to understand that per the Federal Bureau of Prisons (as of June 25th, 2016) forty-six percent (46.4%) of inmates were drug offenders (84,746 prisoners) so far.

When we combine these figures, we see that approximately thirty-seven thousand (36,864) of those were Black American men. Since we know the primary reason behind these crimes are because of economic disparity in the black community we can conclude that the prison industry is exploiting poor Black Americans for profit. We cannot, with a good conscience support these endeavors.

While I do not condone criminal activity of any kind, I also do not condone the exploitation of criminal activity either. There is a "Love/Hate Triangle" between Black Americans, the major companies they patronize and the prisons those companies use for profit.

Black Americans coming up in low income areas are faced with the higher probability of committing and being convicted of a crime, which builds these companies' slave workforces. Black Americans then work and shop at these stores (more than any other group in the United States) which naturally allows the companies to build even more wealth. So, we have a company that profits from every aspect of Black America; the inmates, the employees and the customers.

Imagine the money you would roughly have if you never bought food from a major fast food restaurant in your life. I'm sure the number is quite high no matter what your income level is. Imagine what you would do with the money if you had it. Imagine how much money in the last 30 years Black Americans have spent on items like that.

Imagine what we could have accomplished as a people if we boycotted the fast food chains from the beginning and used the freed funds to build our communities up. This is the frame of mind that will get Black Americans where we need to be as a collective, moving forward.

Maybe if Black Americans saved and invested in their communities instead of shopping at huge department stores the likelihood of Black Americans committing and being convicted of a crime would decrease, reducing the number of Black Americans who are being exploited for profit.

Again, these companies or any company, in general, cannot survive without consistent patronage, so this is not an outlandish claim. For the sake of a powerful boycotting movement, Black Americans must understand how our dollars are necessary to maintain the status quo in the United States and consequently even abroad.

Whether the method is to do it loudly or quietly, the boycotting of unethical businesses by Black America is absolutely a vital piece of our economic empowerment. We have a hard time building wealth in Black America because we vigorously spend it outside of our communities as soon as we get it, those stores usually being the ones profiting from slave labor. It is our responsibility to take charge of our dollars and stop funding our own oppression and start supporting our own liberation.

As stated in the Clothing & Apparel section, our goods do not have to be made in unethical ways, no matter what it is. Whether it be electronics or toiletries, textiles or clothing, our goods should not be made at the expense of poor men, women and children slaving away in a sweatshop or prison. Instead, we can gainfully employ our population to make these things and ethically outsource jobs for people abroad to help manufacture them. It must be widely understood and practiced that these forms of production are no longer accepted in America.

Boycotting reminds everyone from the consumer to the producer of the real power of supply and demand. People must understand that these businesses cannot operate in the capacity that they are without the dollars we spend with them.

If we are truly against unethical business practices, then we must back those sentiments up with economic action and withhold our funds from their accounts. This provokes change in a system that has long been the profiteers of these endeavors. The Montgomery Bus Company couldn't operate without Black American dollars and because of this bent to the whims of their customer base and made a change in policy.

We cannot afford to underestimate the power of boycotting in the perspective of economic growth. So, whenever Black Americans boycott a business, we will have a community business to supplement and be used instead. For instance, all the money that the Montgomery bus company would normally get in a year was going to black taxi cab businesses and black private drivers. Boycotting is much more than not shopping with a business; it's a political, economic statement; saying that we as a people have a set of common cultural standards, morals, values, and beliefs and we do not support anything that goes against that.

These shared cultural standards promote self-sustainability among the people in which they largely produce all the things they want and need. Of course, it is open to the world market, but its primary function is to make sure all the lives connected to it are taken care of. Boycotting is not race specific. Anybody of any ethnic background can be boycotted if not aligned with people's standards. If businesses want our dollars, then they must offer and provide the things we desire to do so, within reason. This is something that has long been subtracted from the minds of most Americans.

Advertising and marketing strategists know that displaying their products, no matter how frivolous, as essentials or necessities is the best way to get attention and sales. This, in turn, means the company that is selling the product is also considered a necessity to the people that shop there.

Even though these businesses need our consistent patronage to stay open, they market themselves as the ones that are required. Consumers subscribe to this notion every time they make a purchase. I've talked to countless people that speak on how they "couldn't live" without a particular good or service and it honestly leaves me perplexed.

On one hand, I do not believe that most of the material goods that are marketed are things we can't live without, but on the other, I do understand the psychology of advertising and marketing. Companies want to showcase the importance of their products and what better way to do it than to make people believe they absolutely need to buy it?

Still, I think a lot of consumers are disillusioned to the point that they will forego their own common sense and compromise their best interests for the chance to spend money. I briefly touched on an aspect of this through the perspective of Black America in the introduction. During segregation, it was a big goal for Black Americans to be able to patronize white owned stores which made it very clear that they did not want black customers. "**WHITES ONLY**" signs flooded storefront windows and sidewalks.

In these times, a lot of White American business owners did not want anything to do with black people and if they did they wanted conflict and violence. In response, Black Americans fought tooth and nail to gain access to these places to spend their hard-earned money with people who apparently hated them.

It was programmed in Black American minds through many psychological factors, the most prevalent being reverse psychology and social exclusion that white owned businesses were the best businesses to be able to patronize.

So, despite them only wanting whites in their stores, Black Americans felt it was a goal to be able to be "accepted" in these places, even if it was just a coffee diner. Even further, I believe since they were not allowed in these establishments it made Black Americans want to be let in even more. Black Americans won the access to these places, but the hatred didn't subside, if anything it might have exacerbated it. Imagine if by law you were forced to serve someone you didn't like. No matter how ignorant the reason, you are not going to take a liking to that other person suddenly just because he or she is now legally obligated to sit next to you.

Now, I won't say that I agree with everything about segregation. I will never champion disrespect, violence or any outward acts of hatred from anyone to anyone, but what I do agree with was the notion of keeping the Black American and other economies separate if there couldn't be a mutual respect between them.

I would have advised against Black Americans fighting to get into racist white owned stores and suggested a boycott which would've saved us the monies necessary to build the equivalents in our own communities to patronize. This way we do not have to subject ourselves to racism and violence while also creating wealth in our own neighborhoods. This allows for a space where non-racist citizens can safely and happily shop as well.

Integration isn't innately bad either. When a mixture of different people come together to live and work in harmony based on commonalities it works very well. I believe that most Black Americans during the times of segregation thought this would be the reality of desegregation. I believe they thought once it was legal to merge communities that black and white people would live in harmony for the general greater good of this country. And truthfully some of these things have and do happen in present times, no doubt.

As we can see, most of the Black American communities are in low income areas. Black Americans have the least jobs, the least amount of household wealth, the least education, the least health standards and the least political representation. This is because even though segregation as a law isn't in place, people of all ethnic backgrounds still primarily rely on themselves in their communities in America before worrying about others. This means it is going to take Black American businesses to create jobs, Black American financial institutions to facilitate wealth, Black American schools, and colleges to educate our youth, and Black American officials and politicians to represent us in government.

The solutions that come from boycotting is endless. You may be asking *"Well, how long will we be boycotting? Are we ever going to be able to shop at these places again eventually, ethically?"*

First, we shouldn't put a time limit on a boycott. When a company knows how long the boycott will be, they can plan for it like lower prices or offer incentives to get more business from the masses. A continual loss in profit and morale is the primary objective for a boycott. This creates an economic vulnerability that allows for public demands to be made and heeded to by the company.

As Black American consumers we can compile a list of demands that we all require in order for them to count on our dollars. Some of those things may be paying the people they have working livable wages, building factories in the Black American communities to offer livable wage jobs, investing in the community to the benefit of the community, etc.

If these requirements are met, then Black Americans have the choice to patronize with a clear conscience regardless of what we choose.

Conclusion:

The Aftermath

This study of Black American money and building your own wealth is hard but very necessary work. The functions of capitalism, economics, and their laws have long been an uninteresting talking point for Black Americans. I know in my life's journey I rarely heard my peers or elders speaking on economics on a fundamental level.

I never got finance advice or stock tips. I never knew what investing truly meant or how to make passive income. These concepts that many have used for their economic empowerment and financial independence were almost entirely unknown to me and my communities. Even if there were a few outliers in the communities I lived in, they never shared their knowledge with me or anyone that I knew.

Because of this ignorance, I grew up spending all the money I made since I was thirteen years old. In the thirteen years of me generating income, I'm willing to assume that I've spent at least five hundred thousand dollars ($500,000+) and saved or invested less than one percent of it.

If I had started saving and investing my money at thirteen, I would have at minimum of a million dollars of wealth by now. These realizations through learning about building wealth showed me what is possible in the present and in the future. I can't do anything about the irresponsible financial decisions I made in the past, but I can make sure I don't repeat those actions and start to make financial decisions centered around never being poor again in my life.

Even though this book is about the macroeconomics of Black America, we can't ignore the microeconomics of Black American households. Black America will not be what we want it to be until Black Americans become the people we want to be. We must raise the awareness and interest in economics. A society cannot thrive without a solid economic base. Whether it be fiat money, raw materials or just human ingenuity, the exchange of goods and services must be mastered as a science in Black America.

Hyper consumption and bad debt are what most Americans knows when it comes to economics, no matter the income level. Having a high education in finance will serve as a catapult to other changes we need as a people. With firm economics, we will know what funds are required to build infrastructure and then hire people to do so. We will be less likely to waste money on material goods and spend wisely. We will plan, create, fund and operate a plethora of businesses and institutions that cater to the overall development of our people.

Ultimately we are striving to be in the space of absolute control and independence from functions in the current system that leave people in bad debt. What this means is when Black

Americans get paid they use most of their dollars to empower themselves and other Black Americans in their community.

When we keep most of our money in our communities, we as a people will never be poor again because of the constant circulation. Think of the Black American dollar as a train riding in a circle. Even if you missed the train the first time around, you still have a chance to catch it again. Black American business owners will provide goods and services to the public. Those companies will bank with Black American financial institutions adding to their wealth. Those Black American financial institutions will have the assets available to invest in more Black American businesses and establishments.

This cycle is the foundation of group economics, and what many other ethnic groups practice in the United States. There's nothing wrong with looking out for you and your people on an economic level, and I believe the lack of such concern for ourselves is one of the big reasons we are in this current condition.

I do not doubt Black Americans are concerned about our issues on a mental and social level, but the initiation of group economics, the actual solution to our biggest problems, goes largely unused.

As time continues to press on, I do think a lot more Black Americans are becoming aware of this solution and want to see where it goes. Seeing eight thousand Black Americans opening accounts with OneUnited Bank and then going on to increase their assets by ten million dollars ($10,000,000) since the creation of this book is what give me hope for the future of Black American economics. Like I said in the introduction, a trillion dollars is an enormous sum of money that can be used and accumulated with the proper planning and budgeting.

This book's purpose is to be a literary reminder of the importance of what people call "Black Excellence" in the community. Truly highlighting all the past, present and future accomplishments of our population and how they can be expanded on with the money we make and spend every year.

If Black America followed the wealth building budget as a collective, we would save up to two hundred billion dollars ($200,000,000,000) a year and invest the same amount. That's four hundred billion dollars ($400,000,000,000) that Black Americans will have put to the side or invested every year. In just ten years that will have accumulated up to four trillion dollars ($4,000,000,000,000) or more of Black American assets. Think of the possibilities.

We have been taught and conditioned to think less of ourselves to the point that we allow the endless possibilities of the world to pass us by. Generations of poverty, debt, and disparity have left us in a horrible state as a people to the point that it has become a celebrated lifestyle.

We turn on our manmade television, unlock our manmade smartphones and computers to watch and learn about other people making these advances, but rarely achieve anything for ourselves. This is because we've been living in an isolated world of limits. When you're surrounded by poverty, it's extremely hard to fathom the possibility of achieving even the most miniscule of things like a high school diploma. For far too long our people have subscribed to the fact *"this is just the way it is"* and not do anything to change or even ask why. *"Why is it the way it is?"*

Many will say institutional racism and white supremacy. While I agree that racist white Americans terrorized the black community at a time in history, I cannot just accept this as a blanket answer, not in 2016, not anymore. At this point in Black American history, we all have access to the knowledge, capital, and resources necessary to completely reverse our living conditions in the United States and ultimately abroad.

If we know that institutional racism and white supremacy are at the root of the problem, why are we voluntarily funding it? Not only are we willingly supporting it, but we are also funding it at exponentially higher and faster rates than any other ethnic group in the United States, including white people themselves. We must understand that Jim Crow and slavery is over. This is not to make people forget what happened, we should all know the history of this country and our people, and I even encourage people to look at Black History before slavery, it's incredible knowledge.

However, when this history is being used as a tool to keep you in a slave state of mind, then it is not for your benefit to know. If you can learn about the enslavement of your people, see how the American Prison Industry is a form of modern day slavery and still shop at the stores that use these inmates in the same fashion as the slave masters did, what was the purpose of learning that information?

Knowledge without application is a wasted lesson. When we learn new things, it should be accompanied with being able to do something new as well. Being able to just "know" things means nothing if it can't be applied in real time especially when dealing with issues such as poverty, crime, violence and broken families.

These problems are deeper than buzzwords to be used to make a point in an argument. Millions of Black Americans are out there wanting a solution, but not knowing what to do or how to start. Our issues are bigger than hashtags and blog articles.

Our issues are deeper than being able to be the most intellectual person in the room. Our issues are far more pressing than whatever is on television or our phones. Our issues need to be addressed and solved by us first and foremost. Our problems are rooted in economics, and so are the solutions.

I know a lot of people may bc thinking *"Money isn't everything. How can all of our issues be based on economics?"* I understand, money isn't everything. What money is though is a means to an end, saying in order for me to get "x" I need to have a certain amount of money.

In American society, our economics is primarily based on fiat money or "cash" to represent value in something. As you become more financially literate, you will know the importance of other forms of currency that people use. Nothing is free in America and if you want to advance you must either have education, skills, money or all three.

Poor people may have the skills, but without the education or money to fund the cultivation of these skills, it's still a high probability that they will not succeed. Even further it's also rare to see poorer classes have individual skills because the lack of money hinders them from building institutions that would facilitate those skills and improve upon them.

The cycle of lacking creates a pathology in the mind of people that leaves them in a perpetual state of mental poverty. More crimes are committed, more acts of violence, more broken homes, more of the same garbage we know in our hearts are wrong and been tired of for generations. All of this is due in large part to poor economic choices and financial illiteracy.

I assure you once we get our economics in order, civil order will follow suit and work. Is it going to be a place where everyone is perfect, and nobody does anything bad anymore? Of course not. But what it will be is a place that has a higher standard of living, so if something like violence or robbery happens, it's appalling and rare because we as people are no longer without wealth.

Criminals who commit crimes just for the hell of it are going to continue to no matter what, but what we can do is make it easier to spot them in the community. When all the people who were committing crimes for the sake of economic distress get off the street and start making legal money, locating an actual criminal will be much easier.

As I've stated before, people are not born criminals; it is a learned behavior, and because of that it can be unlearned and counteracted with new knowledge. If poverty can make people murder their neighbors, then surely poverty can cause domestic violence and broken families. Surely poverty can contribute to the bad health and bad health choices.

Surely poverty can provide miseducation to the youth and slow up their mental and physical development. Surely poverty can cause people to hate one another. Poverty is not just a living condition; poverty is a state of mind. The way people think and live are entirely dictated by their economic status in their society, and if you live in poverty, you will more than likely think and behave in poverty as well.

Therefore, economics is at the root of our problems and solutions. While it would be easier to demand and expect another group of people to "clean up the mess," it is not the reality we live in. If Black Americans want to be free, we must take our freedom in our own hands and never give it back. That is the only way.

All the initiatives I presented in this book was proposed with the betterment of Black American lives and others in mind. At this point in my journey, I am not motivated to "stick it to the man" in the ways that may have been executed in the past. I don't believe we need to put ourselves in harm's way to live a free life.

Don't get me wrong, the ultimate price for freedom is death, and I will always encourage everyone to learn how to defend themselves from any violence that may come their way, but in 2016 the real victory is to become completely self-sustaining and collectively wealthy. We must understand that the abuse of power and position that is used against us is because we don't use the resources allotted to defend ourselves as a people.

Once we build our society up, create our own systems, put our people in positions of authority and circulate our money we will see a decline of injustices against Black Americans. That's the solution I am the most confident in because it does not depend on others to make things happen for us. These initiatives will be majority owned and operated by Black Americans which means we are the source of our liberation and empowerment. When we control the industries we work and shop in, the likelihood of droughts or destitution of a good or service significantly reduces.

I believe every American community that needs developing could use these initiatives and I encourage others to apply them where they see fit. My plans for this book is to inspire the people who want actual change in our lifetime. To show everyone who reads this that there are solutions to the ills we face daily, all it takes is the mindset to make the solutions a reality.

I plan for this book to do its part in ending American poverty. I intend for this book to inspire more books like it. I plan for this book to educate Americans on their real economic power. I plan for this book to encourage people to eat healthier and use nature's medicine before using synthetic drugs. I plan for this book to encourage people to consume less, save and invest more. I plan for this book to be a staple in Black American households and taught to children of all ages.

This book was something I felt I owed my people. I believe that knowledge is meant to be shared with everyone who is willing to listen. For almost 3 years I have been studying and researching these economic aspects of Black American life, and

I had to pass it along in the best way I knew how. This is how knowledge circulates.

Once one family starts to reap the benefits of their newfound knowledge, they will then share the information with their neighbors. The neighbors continue the perpetuation of this information until it becomes a common custom in that community. This changes the landscape of an area for the better. Black American households as a whole will finally know their worth and how to increase it. The objective is to make this behavior second nature in most if not all Black American homes.

What is also taking place is the healing Black Americans as a people have always needed. Changing the economic status of households and the landscape of environments allows Black Americans the clear space to finally be at peace with themselves as a nation.

Not having to stress about money or living in a dangerous neighborhood gives Black

Americans an easier opportunity to deal with personal traumas that have been endured throughout their lives. Since we know everything begins in the mind, improving our mental health is another key ingredient in the recipe for success. The words that people speak literally dictate the life they are going to live. Learn and sharpen your vocabulary to regularly talk about progress and prosperity. If you say you are poor, then you will be.

Being able to settle differences with our neighbors, friends and family will be much easier when everyone involved has more established households. This disconnect we see in the black community today didn't happen overnight. Years and years of systematic miseducation and brutality were used to keep black communities from banding together. Lack of economic opportunities inside the community turned friends into enemies, fighting one another for whatever sources of income were available. Drugs and guns being strategically placed in our communities only made things worse.

Black Americans cannot afford to look at themselves as the lesser of the groups in this country any longer. We are not a desperate oppressed people that can't get ahead because of institutionalized racism and white supremacy, which should not be the narrative of Black America. We are an intuitive, energetic, innovative, adaptable, pioneering, educated and wealthy people that strive for success and prosperity.

Being black in America needs a better look. Where the amazing things Black Americans do are broadcasted and celebrated more than the negative. Where Black Americans respect themselves just as much as they comply with the word and opinions of other groups. Where striving for excellence is a common custom in the community rather than it being an extraordinary occurrence. Where Black Americans unite and come together for common goods instead of in-fighting over differences.

This is what I see for the communities we live in. Throughout my journey, I've been called "unrealistic," "optimistic," "naive" and even downright misinformed for believing Black America could ever be in the position to achieve all the things I've detailed in this book. People told me we would be taken down and bombed like Black Wall Street in Tulsa, Oklahoma in 1921 if we attempt to apply group economics again.

These sentiments don't shake my stance. In fact, they only prove that I am on the right side of history. What many naysayers do not realize is that Black Wall Street residents rebuilt their community and thrived forty more years up until desegregation.

We cannot let tragedies be the only determining factors in our development. Instead let's look at what happened and see what was done right, what was done wrong and how we can improve on it. I don't think many people know the full story of Black Wall Street and its accomplishments.

The story of Black Wall Street is much more than a piece of history where Black Americans were attacked and bombed for being self-sufficient. Black Wall Street was a fantastic example of what we are capable of once we aggregate our skills and funds for the greater good of everyone that participates.

The Greenwood community of Tulsa, Oklahoma was the home of some of the top professional Black Americans in the country. Since its inception in 1830 the neighborhoods were teeming with beautiful homes, thriving businesses and state of the art technology that everyone contributed to.

By the early 1900's the population grew from ten thousand (10,000) people to over one hundred thousand (100,000) because of how attractive and prosperous the city was, continuously expanding the limits of that area to the countryside that surrounded it. Because the city's prosperity came from a local source of oil, Black Americans opened over four hundred different oil and gas companies throughout the area.

Black Wall Street was considered the "Oil capital of the world" and because of that Black Americans also built manufacturing plants, refineries and other utility businesses that catered to their development through this natural resource. Black Wall Street's infrastructure was incredible as well. Black Americans built four different railroads and two separate inner city train systems.

They built a City Hall, a Federal building, a commercial airport and even a bridge that stretched over the Arkansas River. Black Americans also built schools, parks, courthouses, a 3,500-seat auditorium and seven different banks that had assets of more than a million dollars each ($13,465,810 each when adjusted for inflation, a total of $94,260,670).

Economics and financial literacy as we can suspect were a major part of the growth of Black

Wall Street. A barrage of investment advisers, stocks and bonds brokerages, real estate agencies, accounting firms, and insurance companies covered the city. These businesses kept Black Americans up to date and knowledgeable about their money and what it could be used for to sustain their livelihoods and accumulate wealth over time.

I put an emphasis on this aspect of Black American life because it shows that the only way to secure wealth in a community is through having people being able to educate the masses on the subject. These institutions were the heartbeat and lifeblood of Black Wall Street because they were where the money the community accumulated was stored.

These systems offered goods and services that further helped the residents make the best financial decisions possible for their households, which ultimately translated to the betterment of the city at large once accounted for as a collective.

Black Wall Street thrived because of financial literacy and the application of group economics.

Every business that you can imagine were around in the early 1900's; you can bet Black Wall Street offered it to the public.

"Frequently awash in money, the citizens of Tulsa had plenty of places to spend it from furniture stores, jewelry shops, and clothing stores to restaurants and cafes, motion picture theaters, billiard halls, and speakeasies. Those who could afford it could find just about anything in Tulsa, from the latest in fashion to the most modern home appliances, including vacuum cleaners, electric washing machines and Victrolas. For those whose luck had run dry, the city had its share of pawnshops and secondhand stores."

- Scott Ellsworth, BlackWallStreet.Org, 2008

The Greenwood communities of Tulsa, Oklahoma were the epitome of what this book describes for Black America, for that time. Poverty, crime, and violence were extremely low, and productivity and wealth were very high. The communities were overrun with beautiful architecture and lush landscaping.

People were proud of where they lived and did everything they could to preserve the integrity of their neighborhoods. Patronizing one another's businesses was a part of their lifestyles which means the people were united in their endeavors. These events took place over one hundred years ago and even though it was attacked, an unspoken factor to the destabilization of the city was the introduction of an integrated society.

Imagine for one moment that your communities and businesses were attacked and bombed, destroying a considerable portion of the development made by you, your family and neighbors. Imagine then coming together for the reconstruction of your society and getting it back to functioning at full capacity. Now imagine laws being passed that allowed the same people that terrorized your community to open their own businesses and institutions in your neighborhoods without any resolution to the past conflicts. And finally, imagine your neighbors, friends and family members flocking to shop with those same people, relinquishing all the economic power they once had almost entirely.

This is what happened in Tulsa, and I'm sure we can all see what was done right, what was done wrong and how we can improve on it for the future. Moving forward Black Americans must have a stronger sense of pride of self to keep from falling in the same economic and social traps we've fallen for over the years. Black Americans have got to stick to their guns when it comes to their development and not be deterred by any possibly deceptive incentives from other groups.

Those who genuinely want to do business with Black Americans will do so, but we must be vigilant against people of any race who are out to exploit, infiltrate and/or destroy the things we have built. Black Americans must have a stronger sense of self preservation and self-defense. Black America must be able to fight back when faced with conflict, from my research this has been something that their enemies were able to take advantage of for a very long time

These types of strategies have been used against us long enough for us to identify it when it happens in present times. The opposition doesn't always mean violent offenses. Sometime your enemy can come in the form of a friend with ulterior motives. We must be mindful of these strategies and work to make sure that they fail in dividing and conquering black people ever again. Self-defense is the real solution, on a mental and physical level. We must be equipped to fight off the enemy by any means necessary.

Defending ourselves from our enemies is something that Black Americans need to practice more of. For far too long Black Americans have been victims of insane amounts of violence and policy from society with little amounts of retaliation in kind. This also needs to be changed. It is completely legal to defend ourselves from an enemy; it is a God given right. We do not have to just to accept our fate as poor, meek black people in this country and be the punching bag of other groups. We can absolutely bear arms in defense of our livelihoods and should if we are being met with that type of resistance. We can also defend ourselves on a political level by having people in official positions to carry out legislation in our favor.

Black Americans aren't a ragtag group of individuals who scrape the bottom of the barrel for a leg up in society. Black Americans aren't an oppressed people that are complacent in the current conditions they are placed in. Black Americans are not people that just accepts the status quo of society and do what they are told. History has shown that black people's biggest Achilles heel was the inability to thwart off invaders, especially in times where they weren't as united as they should be. Overwhelming firepower and violence bullied people into submission and perpetuated through time to the point we believe other people are inherently superior to us.

Therefore, creating our own police and military force is critical. Black Americans should not have an agenda to attack anyone offensively, but they should be prepared to protect their best interests at any given moment and defend themselves.

Our officers will also be soldiers for Black America, protecting our communities from any people that have the intention to harm us for any reason. Manufacturing our own weaponry shouldn't be something that Black Americans shy from because of the stigma it may place on our people.

We will have finally answered the age-old question of *"who polices the police?"* through our own actions of self-defense.

This time around Black Americans will use history and present times to properly execute these initiatives as not to be undone by external groups. No longer will black people just accept what is being told to them at face value. No longer will "outsiders" be allowed access to organizations that cater specifically to blacks. No longer will Black Americans look at White Americans as their superior, but their equals.

In the aftermath of everything we know and see, Black America will be a self-sustaining, self-sufficient, wealthy nation that banded together for the greater good of themselves and the rest of humanity. We have the power to overcome any obstacle and achieve any goal just as long as we stick together and circulate our dollars.

Economics, control, and ownership is the prerequisite to all of this, and that's why keeping our money in our communities plays such an integral role in Black American empowerment. If black people want progression, equality, justice, liberation and freedom, then we must utilize our funds to do so. My book doesn't have all the answers. There is a bunch of research and education that needs to take place to execute these initiatives; this book is here to show everyone they are still affordable, very doable and should be done.

The vision I have for Black America has already been done countless times throughout history; we just have to continue the works and expand on them. Black America will be a place of prosperity, unity, wealth and independence that we all will be proud of. When we apply the initiatives in this book, we will see an almost complete turnaround in the living conditions of Black America. We will see more educated, civil, wealthy and prosperous people in the community. Negative stereotypes will largely be a thing of the past. All our wildest dreams of advancement will finally be realized and not be deterred because of social and economic disparities. When Black Americans execute these initiatives and others, we will finally be free.

Resources:

Black Business Directory

To date, there are over two million Black American owned businesses currently registered in the United States with room for growth. This fact further supports the notion that Black Americans can entirely sustain themselves once they focus their funds in their communities. The relationship between the Black American producer and the global consumer base must be solidified and strengthened by Black American shoppers.

For this relationship to work Black Americans must understand that there are codes of conduct that we must adhere to for the growth of our people. First and foremost, our Black American business owners must provide high quality goods and services throughout their entire establishment. From the CEO to the custodial staff, Black American companies should represent the epitome of their industry's standard and push the boundaries to exceed those standards, setting new ones.

We cannot support businesses that are only out for a quick buck to continue bad business practices; this is a part of the standard. If business owners want to thrive then, they must take pride in their business and do things the right way, or they will inevitably face the same fate of many small firms that scraped at the bare minimum, permanently closing. Throughout my time compiling the list of Black American companies in this section I came across so many failed business ventures. From grocery stores to trucking companies, so many are now closed due to two big reasons: Lack of business and financial literacy and lack of consistent patronage.

As I was doing research on this chapter, a friend of mine, marketing strategist Ali Shakur published an article titled *"Black Businesses: 5 Reasons why they fail and need celebrities"*. In the article, he explains common mistakes black business owners make and some sound solutions as well.

"Black entrepreneurs have to diversify their business portfolios. Create businesses that complement each other. For example, if a black opens a barber shop or hair salon, then why does the Korean man own the beauty supply shop AND the trucking company that makes the deliveries? Blacks need to own the whole supply chain. Look at the market size and research the competition before you decide to open your business. You may find that even if you win, you'll probably barely cover rent and expenses.

Do the math. Try to guesstimate the possible cost structure. Calculate estimated revenue and expenses to see if it's even worth your time. Will it allow you to buy your mom a new house? Two houses and a boat? Private jet? Space

shuttle? Stop copying what your peers are doing and go be innovative. Do something that people rarely do or think about. Be unique and you'll win. If your product isn't unique, find ways to make it unique."

This initiative helps these things by showing entrepreneurs and consumers the importance of having a balanced relationship with one another. These businesses will now cater to their respective customer bases by providing the best customer service and policies that make certain customer satisfaction is a guarantee.

Black American business districts will do their best to offer competitive pricing and promotional incentives to garner the support of our growing consumer base. Competition among successful companies allows the consumer to choose where and how they prefer their wants and needs, which then gives the businesses the opportunity to make changes to broaden their appeal.

We will alter the dynamic of the producer and consumer relationship by employing advertising and marketing strategies that promote a mutual exchange of currency for goods and services. When you provide a high quality good or service, you do not need to use deceptive tactics to trick people into buying into your business. These promotions will add to our consumer bases because they show an honest portrayal of appreciation to the shoppers.

We have been bombarded with media suggesting that the only way to amass wealth in this country is to be a shrewd greedy businessman with a heart of stone that saves every penny. This just isn't true. While being greedy and selfish will allow you to save money because you're only thinking about how you (and only you) can get more than what you have already, this isn't how most people operate.

These business types are only in business because they rely on the complacency of their employees and customers that believe they need the business more than the business needs them. They protect themselves with laws, policies, and money, rarely or never getting in trouble for their actions. Given these circumstances, Black Americans will provide an alternative business type that thrives on positive customer and employee rapport and providing high quality goods and services.

As an American consumer, which would you prefer, a company that goes above and beyond their expectations while offering competitive prices or a business that provides the bare minimum or below average goods and services at relatively low prices? Let's also add the fact that shopping with the former company may ultimately add to your wealth as a collective. I think the answer is quite clear. These are the decisions Black Americans will be faced with when it's time to spend their money. Since we know that Black Americans set the trends in the US retail market, we know that once we start patronizing our businesses so will the rest of the country. This domino effect of consumerism in Black America will be how their companies reach international audiences as well.

Being financially literate producers and consumers are fundamental principles in building a society up. It takes the concerted effort of everyone involved to make it happen. Black American businesses will be providing high quality goods and services, and the consumer bases will frequently shop with them. The reason I know this is possible in the present is because the communities across the nation that are participating in these types of relationships. All around the country small businesses are thriving because of local and national patronage and it's time Black Americans start being involved in these endeavors at higher rates.

What better time than the present? I chose to create a directory of Black American businesses and institutions from some of the sections I wrote in this book that offer high quality goods and services to the public. This way people can refer to this list while also doing their due diligence on other black owned businesses that are in their area. Referring to these lists gives people the option of which business they would like to patronize at their convenience.

A notion that I'm sure of is that most Americans don't know these companies exist. Because of the unpopularity of a lot of these stores, most people will overlook them in pursuit of whatever good or service they are shopping for. It is paramount to understand that businesses can only expand and be greater if the people shops with them.

I also want to let it be known that Black American business owners cannot guilt people into shopping with them just because they are black. "Support Black Business" is a mantra that many people subscribe to and for the most part, I can agree. However, there still must be a universal standard upheld by business owners to garner the patronage of the public. Merely being a black business owner is not enough. In this capitalistic society, companies are relentlessly competing for more of the market share and one of the major things that set companies apart from each other is the quality of their business.

If you are only open for business to “get rich quick” or to quickly turn ten dollars into twenty, then your business won’t last long. Business owners should all have a financial plan on how they are going to operate in the long term (5-10 years plus) and apply those plans to make sure they are in business for as long as possible.

Being a business owner has an extensive list of responsibilities and duties that come with it. It is much more than selling products and making money. We are required to take inventory, manage budgets, build relationships with customers and other businesses, pay wages, study and pay taxes, overhead, and other expenses, seek legal and financial advice and representation, quality checks and customer service, not to mention a lifelong education on how to stay in business and prosper. A lot goes into running a successful business, and one of the main driving forces is the money coming in from frequent shoppers.

So, whether you're a customer, a business owner or both, understand the power you have and use it to the best of your ability at all times. This list was compiled from websites like OfficialBlackWallStreet.com where they provide local and national listings of black businesses. Despite the lack of mainstream advertising, there are millions of Black American businesses that are here to cater to the public.

Food Services

Five Seeds Farm & Apiary

3500 Kenyon Avenue, Baltimore MD 21213

16528 Dubbs Rd, Sparks, MD 21152

(202) 573-7376

Website: www.fiveseedsfarm.com

Truly Living Well

3353 Washington Road East Point, GA 30344

324 Lawton St. SW Atlanta, GA 30310

1856 Harbin Road Atlanta, GA 30311

Route 316 Fayetteville, GA 30214

(678) 973-0997

Website: www.trulylivingwell.com / info@trulylivingwell.com

Your Bountiful Harvest

4451 S Federal St. Chicago, IL 60609

Website: www.yourbountifulharvest.com

Château Hough Vineyard

E. 66th St. and Hough Ave. Cleveland, Ohio 44103

(216) 469-0124

Website/Email: www.chateauhough.org / info@neighborhoodsolutionsinc.com

Rid-All Green Partnership

8129 Otter Road Cleveland, Ohio 44104

(216) 990-8191

Website/Email: www.ridall.org / info@ridall.org

Good Sense Farm & Apiary

Website/Email: www.goodsensefarm.com / info@goodsensefarm.com

Three Part Harmony Farm

Website/Email: www.threepartharmonyfarm.org / info@threepartharmonyfarm.com

Farms to Grow, Inc.

5316 Telegraph Ave, Oakland CA

(510) 379-8600

Website/Email: www.farmstogrow.com / info@farmstogrow.com

People's Grocery

(510) 652-7607

Website/Email: www.peoplesgrocery.org / info@peoplesgrocery.com

Phat Beets Produce

Dover St. Park 5707 Dover St. Oakland, CA

(510) 250-7957

Website/Email: www.phatbeetsproduce.org / info@phatbeetsproduce.org

D-Town Farm

3800 Puritan Detroit, Michigan 48238

(313) 345-3663

Website/Email:

www.dtownfarm.blogspot.com /

info@Detroitblackfoodsecurity.org

SoLA Food Co-Op

(323) 388-5258

Website/Email: www.solafoodcoop.com /

Philly Urban Creators

2315 N 11th St. Philadelphia, PA 19133

Website/Email:

www.phillyurbancreators.org /

admin@phillyurbancreators.org

Mill Creek Farm

4901 Brown Street, Philadelphia, PA, 19123

4919 Pentridge Street, Philadelphia, PA, 19143

(347) 415-0223

Website/Email: www.millcreekurbanfarm.org / millcreekfarmphilly@gmail.com

The BLK ProjeK

928 Intervale Ave Bronx, NY 10459

Website: www.theblkprojek.org

East New York Farms

613 New Lots Avenue Brooklyn, NY 11207

(718) 649-7979

Website/Email: www.eastnewyorkfarms.org / david@eastnewyorkfarms.org

Tiger Mountain Foundation

3146 East Wier Ave, Suite 31 Phoenix, AZ 85040

(602) 687-7725

Website/Email: www.tigermountainfoundation.org darren.chapman@tigermountainfoundation.org

Karyn's

1901 N. Halsted Chicago, Illinois 60614

(312) 255-1590

Website/Email: www.karynraw.com / karyninfo@karynraw.com

Original Soul Vegetarian

203 E. 75th Street Chicago, IL 60619

(773) 496-4680

Website: www.originalsoulvegetarian.com

Khepra's Raw Food Juice Bar

402 H St NE, Washington, DC 20002

(202) 803 2063

Website/Email:
www.khepras rawfoodjuicebar.com /
khepra@khepras rawfoodjuicebar.com

Land of Kush

840 N. Eutaw St. Baltimore, MD 21201

(410) 225-5874

Website: www.landofkush.com

Woodlands Vegan Bistro

2928 Georgia Avenue, NW Washington, DC 20001

(202) 232-1700

Website: www.woodlandsveganbistro.com

Four Seasons Bakery & Juice Bar

2281 Church Ave Brooklyn NY, 11226

(718) 693-7996

Website: www.fourseasonsdelight.com

Strictly Vegetarian Restaurant

2268 Church Ave Brooklyn, NY 11226

(718) 284-2543

Veggie Castle II

13209 Liberty Ave South Richmond Hill, NY 11419

(718) 641-8342

Judahlicious

3906 Judah Street San Francisco, CA 94122

(415) 665-8423

Website/Email: www.judahlicious.com / judahliciousjuice@gmail.com

Free Soul Caffe

191 East Main Street Suite 1B, Tustin, California 92780

(714) 371-0976

Website: www.freesoulcaffe.com

Simply Pure by Chef Stacey Dougan

707 Fremont St Ste #1310 Las Vegas, NV 89101

(702) 810-5641

Website: www.simplypurelv.com

Lov'n It Live

2796 East Point Street East Point, Georgia 30344

(404) 765-9220

Website: www.lovingitlive.com

Healthful Essence

875 York Avenue SW, Atlanta, Georgia 30310

(404) 806-0830

Website: www.healthfulessence.com

Tassili's Raw Reality

1059 Ralph David Abernathy Blvd Atlanta, Georgia 30310□

(404) 343-6126

Website: www.tassilisrawreality.com

Soul Vegetarian Restaurant

879 Ralph David Abernathy Blvd SW Atlanta, GA 30310

(404) 752-5194

652 N Highland Ave NE Atlanta, GA 30306-4533

(404) 875-0145

Website: www.soulvegetarian2.com

Vegan Flava Cafe

4125 Durham Chapel Hill Blvd Durham, NC 27707

(919) 960-1832

Website/Email: www.veganflavacafe.com / info@veganflavacafe.com

Lamb's Bread Vegan Café

2338 Main St. Columbia, SC 29201

(803) 253-7889

Rawtopian Bliss

8502 Two Notch Road, Suite i, Columbia, SC 29223

(803) 518-8927

Website/Email: www.rawtopianbliss.com / chefsaa@rawtopianbliss.org

Soul Veg Tallahassee Restaurant & Catering

1205 South Adams Street, Tallahassee, Florida 32301

(850) 893-8208

Website: www.soulvegtallahassee.com

Educational Services

Marcus Garvey School

5760 6th Avenue Los Angeles, CA. 90043

(323) 294-1020

Website/Email: www.mgsla.org / enrollment@mgsla.org

NationHouse

6101 Dix St NE Washington, DC 20019

(202) 291-5600

Website/Email: www.nationhouse.org / info@nationhouse.org

Timbuktu Academy

10800 E. Canfield St Detroit, MI 48214

(313) 823-6000

Website/Email: www.timbuktuacademy.org / mamenra@timbuktuacademy.org

Betty Shabazz International Charter School

7822 S Dobson Ave Chicago, IL 60619

(773) 651-1221

Website: www.bsics.org

Little Sun People, Inc.

1360 Fulton Street Brooklyn NY 11216

(718)789-7330

Website/Email: www.littlesunpeople.com / info@littlesunpeople.com

Imhotep Institute Charter High School

6201 N 21st Street, Philadelphia, PA 19138

(215) 438-4140

Website/Email: www.imhotepcharter.org / info@imhotepcharter.org

Kamali Academy

New Orleans, LA

(504) 534-5131

Website/Email: www.kamaliacademy.com / KamaliAcademy@gmail.com

Sankofa Freedom Academy Charter School

2501 Kensington Ave, Philadelphia, PA 19125

(215) 288-2001

Website/Email: www.sfacs.us / d.pride@sfacs.us

Urban Prep Academies

420 N. Wabash, Suite 300 Chicago, IL 60611

(312) 276-0259

Website: www.urbanprep.org

Thurgood Marshall Academy

2427 Martin Luther King Jr Ave SE, Washington, DC 20020

(202) 563-6862

Website/Email: www.thurgoodmarshallacademy.org / info@tmapchs.org

A Mother's Care Learning Center

5861 NW 17th Ave, Miami, FL 33142

(305) 696-3802

Greater Expectations Early Child Development & Learning Center Inc.

4981 W. Oglethorpe Hwy. Hinesville, GA 31313

(912) 876-5437

Website: www.greaterexpectations.biz

Our Magic Years Childcare Center

866 Georgetown St, Lexington, KY 40511

(859) 280-9170

Real Estate & Construction

Thor Construction

714 Olympic, Suite 1010 Los Angeles, CA 90015

(855) 461-4048

Website/Email: www.thorcon.net / thormail@thorcon.net

Powers & Sons Construction Company

5040 South State Street Chicago, IL 60609

(773) 536-3100

Website: www.powersandsons.com

The Peebles Corporation

745 Fifth Avenue, 16th Floor New York, NY 10151

(212) 355-1655

Website: www.peeblescorp.com

H.J Russell & Company

171 17th Street NW Suite 1600 Atlanta, GA 30363

(404) 330 1000

Website/Email: www.hjrussell.com / info@hjrussell.com

Omni New York, LLC

885 Second Avenue, 31st Floor New York, NY 10017

(646) 502-7200

Website/Email: www.onyllc.com / info@onyllc.com

Deborah V. Morris, REALTOR

1520 Killearn Center Blvd Tallahassee, Florida 32309 United States

(850) 980-1101

Website/Email: www.deborahvmorris.kw.com / deborahvmorris@kw.com

Northern Real Estate Urban Ventures, LLC

641 S Street, NW Suite 4023 Washington, DC 20001

(202) 460-0468

Website/Email: www.nreuv.com / info@nreuv.com

Real Estate Surveyors & Developers, LLC

8325 Cherry Lane, Laurel, MD 20707

(240) 459-3337

Website/Email: www.resdllc.com / info@resdllc.com

Pacific Real Estate Management Group, Inc.

351 NW 12th Ave Portland, Oregon 97209

(503) 224-1460

RG's House Investments, LLC

11670 Fountain Dr. Suite 200, Maple Grove, Minnesota 55369

(763) 445-2606

Website/Email: www.rgshouse.com / raygivens@rgshouse.info

First Action Realty

6135 Park South Dr,, Suite 510 Charlotte NC 28210

(704) 779-4421

Website: www.firstactionrealtync.com

Brown Realty Group

9250 Laguna Springs Drive, Suite 100 Elk Grove, CA 95758

(916) 956-6061

Website: www.brownrealtygroup.com

Deborah Bernat - Hammond Residential Real Estate

(617) 699-5878

Website: www.deborahbernat.com

Gloria Brown Real Estate Services

5450 Lafayette Road Suite 1 Indianapolis IN 46254

(317) 316-8013

Website/Email: www.indianapolishomesgloriabrown.com / indyhouses4sale@aol.com

Helpful Helen & Associates

2690 Cobb Pkwy. SE Suite A5-333 Smyrna, GA 30080

(404) 933-4017

Website/Email: www.helpfulhelenrealtor.com / helen@helpfulhelenrealtor.com

Jamie Lamartin, Realtor

P.O. Box 12101 Silver Spring, MD 20908

(443) 221-3559

Website/Email: www.jamielamartin.com / jamielamartin@gmail.com

Felder & Company Realtors

8404 Capriola Lane Suite 100 Dallas, TX 75228

(214) 559-6999

Website: www.feldersellshomes.com

DC Home Buzz

1405 Park Rd NW, Washington, DC 20010

(202) 999-3131

Website/Email: www.dchomebuzz.com / info@dchomebuzz.com

Clothing & Apparel

Garb Boutique

2042 Magazine St, New Orleans, LA 70130

(504) 301-9174

Website: www.shopgarbboutique.com

Meow and Barks Boutique

1537 San Marco Blvd, Jacksonville, FL 32207

(904) 704-8222

Website: www.meowandbarksboutique.storenvy.com

Violet Flower Boutique

PO BOX 682751, Franklin, TN 37068

(615) 939-9923

Website/Email: www.violetflower.boutique / violetflowerbtq@gmail.com

Tags Boutique

225, 2140 Peachtree St NW, Atlanta, GA 30309

(404) 883-3836

Website/Email: www.tagsatl.com / orders@tagsatl.com

Michelle New York

376 Atlantic Ave (btw Hoyt & Bond St) Brooklyn, NY 11217

(718) 643-1680

Website/Email: www.michellenewyork.com / info@michellenewyork.com

Harlem Haberdashery

245 Malcolm X Blvd, New York, NY 10027

(646) 707-0070

Website/Email:

www.harlemhaberdashery.com /

info@harlemhaberdashery.com

Murk

Website: www.murkworldwide.com

The Extinct Breed

Website: www.thextinctbreed.bigcartel.com

Always Run Deep

Website: www.alwaysrundeep.com

Nudxty

Website: www.nudxty.com

H33M, Inc.

Website: www.shop.h33minc.com

Ode Clothing

Website: www.odeclothing.com

Roole

Website/Email: www.roole.co / Gordonsholliday@gmail.com

Corner Store Goods

Website: www.cornerstoregoods.us

Creed Co.

Website: www.creedco.net

J. Reid

Website: www.jreid.me

Progression Matters

Website:
www.progressionmatters.bigcartel.com

Peas N Carats International

210 Barton Springs Rd Ste #500 Austin, TX 78704

Website: www.peasncaratsintl.com

Play Cloths

Website: www.playcloths.com

Kosmic Kickz

Website: www.kosmickickz.com

LXXRYSPORT Co.

Website: www.lxxrysportco.bigcartel.com

Advertising/Marketing

Burrell Communications Group, Inc.

20 N. Michigan Avenue Chicago, IL 60602

(312) 443-8600

Website/Email: www.burrell.com / fferguson@burrell.com

UniWorld Group, Inc.

1 MetroTech Center, Brooklyn, NY 11201

(212) 219-1600

Website/Email: www.uwg.is / newbiz@uwg.is

GlobalHue

440 9th Avenue 8th FL.

New York, New York 10001

(646) 871-6200

Website/Email: www.globalhue.com / info@globalhue.com

Carol H. Williams Advertising

(510) 763-5200

Website/Email: www.carolhwilliams.com / tellmemore@carolhwilliams.com

Images USA

1320 Ellsworth Industrial Blvd. Bldg C Atlanta, GA 30318

(404) 892-2931

Website/Email: www.imagesusa.net / B.McNeil@imagesusa.net

Entertainment

Nerjyzed Entertainment

447 Third Street, Suite 200, Baton Rouge, LA 70802

(225) 395-1844

Website/Email: www.nerjyzed.com / info@nerjyzed.com

Atom Factory

10351 Washington Blvd, Culver City, CA 90232

(310) 828-7200

Website: www.atomfactory.com

Radio One, Inc.

1010 Wayne Ave. 14th Floor Silver Spring, MD 20910

(301) 429-3200

Website/Email: www.radio-one.com / info@radio-one.com

Sports & Recreation

Coast to Coast Football

3317 S. Higley Road, Suite 114-230 Gilbert, Arizona 85297

(480) 988-0641

Website/Email: www.coast2coastfootball.com / info@coast2coastfootball.com

BRUKWINE

520 8th Ave, 16th Floor New York, NY 10018

45 4th Ave Brooklyn, NY 11217

Website: www.brukwine.com

Black Girls RUN!

Website: www.blackgirlsrun.com

Black Men RUN!

Website/Email: www.blkmenrun.com / info@blkmenrun.com

KTX Fitness

3201 MLK Jr. Dr. SW, Atlanta, GA 30311

(404) 797-5630

Website/Email: www.ktxfitness.com / keith@ktxfitness.com

SolBox Fitness Club

7101 N. Miami Ave, #107 Miami, FL 33150

(305) 759-7685

Website/Email: www.solboxfitnessclub.com / solboxfitnessclub@gmail.com

All Pro Sports & Entertainment, Inc.

36 Steele Street, Suite 100 Denver, CO 80206

(303) 320-4004

Website: www.apse.net

JayLo Fitness

6910 Snowden Ln Southaven, MS 38671

(901) 619-5662

Website/Email: www.jaylofitness.com / jaylo@jaylofitness.com

Tiffany Rothe FitClub

Website: www.icfc.club

J.J. Smith

12138 Central Ave Suite 391 Mitchellville, MD 20721

(202) 558-5543

Website/Email: www.jjsmithonline.com / info@jjsmithonline.com

Mr. Shut Up & Train

500 Bishop St NW, Atlanta, GA 30318

Website/Email: www.mrshutupandtrain.com / info@mrshutupandtrain.com

Be the Better with Barrington

Website: www.bethebetter.com

Locale Village Shop & Yoga

410 Marcus Garvey Blvd, Brooklyn NY 11216

(347) 318-3031

Website/Email: www.locale.nyc / info@locale.nyc

Work Hard Train Harder

301 W 135th St, 2nd Fl New York, NY 10030

(872) 222-9484

Website/Email: www.workhardtrainharder.com / pj@workhardtrainharder.com

Move with Grace

431 Myrtle Ave, Brooklyn, NY 11205

(718) 230-0013

Website: www.movewithgrace.com / info@movewithgrace.com

Lafemme Suite

2364 Adam Clayton Blvd. New York, NY 10030

(917) 507-9475

Website/Email: www.lafemmesuite.com / contact@lafemmesuite.com

Ailey Extension

405 W 55th Street, New York, NY 10019

(212) 405-9000

Website: www.aileyextension.com

Punch Fitness Center

1015 Madison Avenue New York, NY 10075

(212) 288-2375

Website/Email: www.punchfitnesscenter.com / madison@punchfitnesscenter.com

Rad Experience

Website: www.radexperience.com

Pace for Success & Fit Factory NYC

153 West 27th Street Ste 201 & 203 New York, NY 10001

(212) 206-7652

Website: www.pace4success.fitness

BellFitness

2400 N. 2ND Street Suite 411 Minneapolis, MN 55411

(952) 334-8954

Website/Email: www.bellfitnesslife.com / jojo@bellfitnesslife.com

BodyRoc

641 New Park Ave, West Hartford, CT 06110

(860) 830-9321

Website/Email: www.bodyrocfitlab.com / Info@BodyRocFitLab.com

Embrace Yoga DC

1650 Columbia Road, NW, 2nd Floor Washington, DC 20009

Website: www.embracedc.com

Evolution Yoga NC

Harrisburg, NC 28075

(704) 776-5867

Website: www.evolutionyoganc.com

Fit4Dance

154 Utica Ave Brooklyn, NY 11213

(347) 921-2404

Website/Email: www.fit4dancenyc.com / info@fit4dancenyc.com

Gymnetics Fitness

1465 Chattahoochee Ave Suite 700, Atlanta, GA 30318

(678) 705-7581

Website: www.gymneticsfitness.com

Harlem Cycle

2350 Adam Clayton Powell New York, NY 10030

(646) 404-2891

Website/Email: www.harlem-cycle.com / info@harlem-Cycle.com

So Hum Studios

(646) 623-6751

Website: www.sohumstudios.weebly.com

SpeedDoctorz2, LLC

(614) 306-6588

Website/Email: www.speeddoctorz2.com / mason@speeddoctorz2.com

Spiritual Essence Yoga

5020 Brown Station Road #130 Upper Marlboro, Maryland 20772

(301) 574-FLOW (3569)

Website/Email: www.spiritualessenceyoga.com / info@spiritualessenceyoga.com

Vibe Ride

950 W Peachtree St NW Suite 225 Atlanta, GA 30309

(470) 225-6195

Website/Email: www.theviberide.com / info@theviberide.com

Wired Cycling DC

2028 4th Street NE Washington, DC

(202) 400-1340

Website: www.wiredcycling.com / letilong@wiredcyclingdc.com

Yoga Hive Healing Art Studios

1001 Virginia Ave, #202 Atlanta, GA 30354

(404) 668-2169

Website/Email: www.yogahive.org / yogahive@gmail.com

YogaLove

3851 Market Street, Oakland, CA 94608

(510) 435-2798

Website/Email: www.yogaloveoakland.com / yogaloveoakland@gmail.com

JamzFit Club

520 8th Avenue, New York, NY 10018

Website/Email: www.jamzfitclub.com / chance@jamzfitclub.com

Transportation Services

The Bulldog Group, LLC

10610 Rhode Island Ave, Suite 301 Beltsville, MD

(240) 839-7018

Website: www.thebulldoggroupllc.com

Ball & Breckenridge Trucking

4627 Breckenridge Ln, Pikesville, MD 21208

(410) 496-2255

Copeland Trucking

5400 NE Main St., Suite 201 Minneapolis, MN 55421

1-800-486-1552

Website/Email: www.copelandtruc-king.com / info@copelandtruc-king.com

Dansville Hauling Corporation

14500 Neale Dr, Brandywine, MD 20613

(301) 372-6431

Denang's Trucking, LLC

12138 Central Avenue, Suite 977, Mitchellville, Maryland 20721

(202) 575-1129

Website/Email: www.denangstruckingllc.com / info@denangstruckingllc.com

Kevin Dockett Sr. Trucking, Inc.

4871 Stamp Rd, Temple Hills, MD 20748

(301) 423-4447

Elite Hauling Group, Inc.

7601-A Barbara Lane, Clinton MD 20735

(301) 868-4811

Website/Email: www.elitehaulinggroup.com / inquiries@elitehaulinggroup.com

G & W Trucking Corporation

4333 Seidel Ave, Baltimore, MD 21206

(410) 325-1372

K Neal International & Idealease

5000 Tuxedo Rd, Hyattsville, MD 20781

(301) 772-5111

Kelley's Trucking, LLC

Sparks, MD

(443) 621-5232

Website/Email:
www.kelleystruckingllc.com /
Keithkelley@kelleystruckingllc.com

LogNet Worldwide

5226 N. Sam Houston Pkwy East Houston, TX 77032

(281) 449-5067

Swift Services

6621 Long Point Rd Houston, TX 77055

(713) 957-8882

Website: www.swiftservices.net

Together We Serve, LLC

14630 Edgemont St, San Antonio, TX 78247

(210) 687-2906

DeLoatch Transportation, Inc.

532 N Regional Rd # B, Greensboro, NC 27409

(336) 294-7800

Hayes Transportation & Logistics, LLC

1001 S. Marshall St, Winston-Salem, NC 27101

(336) 575-2982

Website/Email: www.hayestran.com / buddy@hayestran.com

R & R Transportation, Inc.

4415 Abner Place Greensboro, NC 27407

(336) 292-4630

Website/Email:
www.rrtransportationinc.com /
info@rrtransportationinc.com

Capital Transportation, Inc.

1170 North Cassady Avenue, Columbus, OH 43219

(614) 258-0400

Website: www.capital-trans.com

Checker Cab of Jacksonville

Jacksonville, FL 32207

(904) 345-3333

Website: www.checkercabofjax.com

Elite Parking Services of America

76 S Laura St, Jacksonville, Florida 32202

(904) 297-4437

Website/Email: www.eliteparkingofamerica.com / info@eliteparkingofamerica.com

Atlanta Peach Movers

2911 Northeast Parkway Atlanta, Georgia 30360

(770) 447-5121

Website: www.atlpeachmovers.com

Imperial Transportation PBC, Inc.

3114 45th St #10, West Palm Beach, FL 33407

(561) 689-3663

Website/Email: www.imperialtrips.com / info@imperialtrips.com

MooreCars, LLC

3800 S Congress Avenue, Suite 8, Boynton Beach, FL 33426

(844) 265-4642

Railroad Industries Incorporated

1575 Delucchi Lane #106 Reno, NV 89502

(775) 329-4855

Website/Email: www.railroadindustries.com / RII@railroadIndustries.com

Tomlin Transportation Consulting, Inc.

P.O. Box 973133 Miami, FL. 33197-3133

(305) 431.7257

Financial Services

Raymond Saylor CPA

26 Court Street Suite 810 Brooklyn, NY 11242

718-858-6808

Website/Email: raysaylorcpapc.com / raysaylorcpa@gmail.com

Chuks L. Iheke Accountancy Corporation

39270 Paseo Padre Pky Suite #250 Fremont, CA 94538-1616

(510) 468-4623

Website/Email: www.clicpa.com / ciheke@clicpa.com

Harris Tax & Financial Solutions

8939 S Sepulveda Blvd. Suite 102, Los Angeles, CA 90045

(310) 242-6420

Website: www.harristaxandfinancials.com

Stanton W. Jones & Associates

57 Post St # 713, San Francisco, CA 94104

(415) 399-1013

Austin Wealth Specialists

1106 Clayton Ln, Austin, TX 78723

(512) 302-5534

Website: www.austinwealthspecialists.net

Britts & Associates, LLP

3201 Cherry Ridge, Ste A104, San Antonio, TX 78230

(210) 735-9101

Website: www.cpasatx.com

The Fly Financial, LLC

New York, NY

Website/Email: www.theflyfinancial.wixsite.com/reserve / theflyfinancial@gmail.com

B&M Financial Management Services, LLC

119 Pondfield Rd, Box 431 Bronxville, NY 10708

(888) 524-4094

Website/Email: www.bmfms.com / info@bmfms.com

ComproTax, Inc.

4155 W Cardinal Drive Beaumont, TX 77705

(409) 832-3266

Website/Email: www.comprotax.net / Compro5Star@gmail.com

National Association of Black Accountants

7474 Greenway Center Drive, Suite 1120 Greenbelt, Maryland 20770

301-474-6222

Website/Email: www.nabainc.org / customerservice@nabainc.org

Lifeway Insurance Brokers

2600 S Loop West Suite 475H, Houston, TX 77054

(281) 232-5207

Website/Email: www.lifeway-insurance.com / brokers@lifeway-insurance.com

Bright Future Credit Solutions

100 Chesterfield Business Pkwy Suite 200, Chesterfield, MO 63005

(877) 799-8699

Website/Email: www.brightfuturecreditsolutions.com / info@brightfuturecreditsolutions.com

Okafor & Associates

3000 Joe DiMaggio Blvd. Building 1400, Suite 52 & 53, Round Rock, TX 78664

(512) 244-4908

Website/Email: www.okaforcpa.com / info@okaforcpa.com

Peter Ejirika Certified Public Accounting & Management Consulting Firm

7901 Cameron Road, Suite 3-307, Austin, TX 78754

(512) 368-0262

Website: www.ejirikacpa.com

OneUnited Bank

3683 Crenshaw Blvd. Los Angeles, CA 90016

(877) 663-8648

Website: www.oneunited.com

Carver Federal Savings Bank

75 West 125th Street New York, NY 10027

(718) 230-2900

Website/Email: www.carverbank.com / customer.service@carverbank.com.

City National Bank

382 West 125th Street Harlem, NY 10027

(212) 865-4763

Website: www.citynatbank.com

United Bank of Philadelphia

30 S 15th Street, Philadelphia PA, 19102

(800) 472-3272

Website/Email: www.ubphila.com / unitedbank@ubphila.com

The Harbor Bank of Maryland

25 W. Fayette Street Baltimore, Maryland 21201

(410) 528-1800

Website: www.theharborbank.com

Industrial Bank

4812 Georgia Avenue, N.W. Washington, D.C. 20011

(202) 722-2000

Website/Email: www.industrial-bank.com / info@industrial-bank.com

Greater Kinston Credit Union

901 N. Queen St. Kinston, NC 28501

(252) 527-4002

Website: www.greaterkcu.org

First Legacy Community Credit Union

431 Beatties Ford Rd. Charlotte, NC 28216

(704) 375-5781

Website: www.firstlegacyccu.org

Credit Union of Atlanta

670 Metropolitan Parkway Atlanta, GA 30310

(404) 658-6465

Website/Email: www.cuatlanta.org / beheard@cuatlanta.org

Alamerica Bank

2170 Highland Ave, Birmingham, AL 32505

(205) 558-4600

Seaway Bank

645 E. 87th Street Chicago, IL 60619

(773) 487-4800

Website/Email: www.seawaybank.us / feedback@seawaybank.us

Illinois Service Federal Savings and Loan Association

4619 S King Dr, Chicago, IL 60653

(773) 624-2000

Website: www.isfbank.com

St. Louis Community Credit Union

3651 Forest Park Ave. St. Louis, MO 63108

(314) 534-7610

Website/Email:

www.stlouiscommunity.com /

info@stlouiscommunity.com

Mount Olive Baptist Church Federal Credit Union

514 N. L. Robinson Drive, Arlington, TX 76011

(817) 261-9325

Website: www.mobcfcu.com

Faith Cooperative Federal Credit Union

2020 West Wheatland Road Dallas, Texas 75232

(972) 228-5222

Website: www.faithcfcu.com

Oak Cliff Christian Federal Credit Union

1130 W. Camp Wisdom Road Dallas, TX 75232

(214) 672-9180

Website: www.occfcu.org

Melvin Securities, LLC

111 W Jackson Blvd # 2110, Chicago, IL 60604

(312) 341-0050

Website: www.melvinco.com

Creative Investment Research, Inc.

624 S Street, NW, Washington, DC, United States, 20001

(202) 455-0430

Website: www.creativeinvest.com

Doss Technical Services

1010 S. Joliet Street, Suite #105, Aurora Colorado 80012

(303) 831-1930

Website/Email: www.dosstechnical.com / info@dosstechnical.com

SDG Financial Services, LLC

663 W. 5th St. 28th Floor, Los Angeles, CA 90071

(213) 223-2207

Website: www.sdgfinancialservices.com

Williams, Adley & Company

1030 15th Street, NW Suite 350 West, Washington, DC 20005

(202) 371-1397

Website: www.williamsadley.com

King Tax Savannah

4012 Montgomery St, Savannah, GA 31405

(912) 376-9484

Website/Email: www.kingtaxsavannah.com / taxprep@kingtaxsavannah.com

Message to the Trillion Dollar Nation

My people. For centuries, we as Black Americans have been through a lot, to say the least. We have had some of the worst behaviors known to mankind acted upon us, and the psychological effects still convey themselves to this day. I completely understand what this country has done to us as a people and will never make an excuse for those atrocious actions. I sometime can't believe the things I read and see on what this country has done to Black Americans. The list is extensive and gets more violent and barbaric the further in history you study.

Despite having all these things happen to us, Black Americans have pushed forward and built ourselves up to the point that we make up most this country's retail market as consumers. Being that this country is predominantly based on the freedom of free trade and commerce, we must start looking at our position in this nation from an economic perspective rather than a social one. For generations, we have been mainly focused on social integration and the inclusion of black people in white ran systems, mostly believing that all our problems would be solved if whites gave blacks a piece of the pie and worked together in harmony.

I mean, the black labor that went into baking that pie plainly grants them their share. In a perfect world, this makes absolute sense and the humanitarian in me wishes that could happen. The truth is this world is the furthest thing from perfect, and we must have a full understanding of the laws of the land to make sure we know how to deal with any injustice that may come our way.

In our quest for the equality and social justice from White Americans, we began neglecting our own communities more and more. It seems paradoxical because the struggle was trying to stop the tyranny whites brought on blacks in this country, but the problem was we were trying to get them to stop by appealing to their better judgement. Showing in a lot of instances that we were not a threat and we just wanted peace.

Even though we have admirable Black Militant groups like the Black Panther Party for Self Defense, they pale in comparison to organizations like the Civil Rights Movement whose deep roots in the Christian church mainly influenced and encouraged the passive approach to freedom.

These peaceful methods are noble, but unrealistic when dealing with people that are that aggressively against their lives. Especially when we see the violent conflicts that happen in our own communities. While Black Americans are peacefully protesting brutality against their people by whites, black men and women are being just as, if not more violent toward each other at alarming rates. We are killing ourselves and justify it by blaming white supremacy, but then treat suspected white supremacists with enough respect that we don't cause them harm. This lack of unity and understanding amongst Black Americans has hurt us in a tremendous way. To the point that drawing these parallels is perceived as deflecting or victim blaming. That is not my intent. My point is that Blacks Americans, for the most part have been looking at the solution all wrong in recent history.

The true solutions have been illustrated in this book: group economics, civil togetherness, love, and unity. In practicing these principles, Black Americans will have the resources and the strength in numbers to seek and obtain justice for the things that other groups have done to us in history.

We must take care of the problems that are closest to home before we can face an outside enemy. If a troop is at odds, they will be of no use on the battlefield. Black Americans must come together again so we can finally stop the perpetuation of being oppressed in this country.

There are some things that I've personally done in my life to change my way of thinking that I believe can help millions of people if they applied it as well. These new things took me, a person who grew up hating reading and math to write a book about business and money. New things that opened my eyes to a lifestyle I never knew existed for people like me.

These things were:

Turning off the TV
Uniting my household
Living a Plant Based lifestyle
Saving and investing more than I spend
Meditating
Writing my thoughts, goals and affirmations down
Reading and studying regularly
Yoga and exercising
Taking breaks from social media
Starting a business
Growing my own food

Connecting with likeminded individuals

Since implementing these new principles in my life, I have seen an abundant increase of health, wealth, and prosperity. I am now engaged to a beautiful woman who I run our family business with. My two daughters are being raised to be amazing young women. I've lost tremendous weight and have never been this healthy ever before.

I am surrounded by people who work and strive to be the best they can be. I even make meals out of the food I grow in my backyard. While life is always filled with hardships and challenges, I am grateful that I have the mental capacity and the physical ability to learn from them and grow as a person. After experiencing the positive changes that these new principles brought I could never go back to the old life I was once living.

In closing, I want everyone reading this to know that there is a solution to all the problems we face in the world today. Even though it may not seem like it, all the things that we go through happen to teach us a lesson. I was broke and angry before I found there was a solution to my problems. I will never act like these solutions are the easiest to implement, but they are worth it in the long run. I wrote this book because I saw there was a need for some guidance and suggestion when it came to the pursuit of the American Dream for black people.

While this book couldn't describe every single detail of these solutions, it still serves as a reference for what is possible with the right amount of education and capital. Black America has the potential to be the leading example of what a unified nation looks like, once we tap into the sections I described in this book and others that weren't mentioned.

We as Black Americans owe it to ourselves and our predecessors to put forth a relentless, unwavering effort to become independent, prosperous people. *Black America, Inc.: A Trillion Dollar Nation* is here as a literary resource to help

Black Americans identify the problems we face and how to begin to solve them. Thank you for your time.

Acknowledgments

First and foremost, I want to acknowledge all the research groups, businesses, and institutions that I gathered my data from. The American Cancer Association, National Restaurant Association, PBS, Congressional Black Caucus Foundation, United States Department of Education, National Home Education Research institute, Bureau of Labor Statistics, International Cotton Advisory Committee, Center on Education and the Workforce at Georgetown, National Center for Education Statistics, Entertainment Software Association, Tech Insights, Inc., Plunkett Research, Ltd., Athletic Business Media, Inc., American Public Transportation Association, The Wall Street Journal, United States Department of Justice, National Fire Protection Agency, Fire Brigades Union, Brass Knuckle Finance University, United States Department of Agriculture, Experian

Information Solutions, Inc., Huffington Post, Demos, NAACP and the Federal Bureau of Prisons.

I want also to acknowledge Damon Kirk, Ali Shakur, Khemmy Flowers, Dr. Sebi, Dr. Llaila Afrika, Queen Afua, Dr. Claude Anderson, Dr. Boyce Watkins and Brotha Polight for inspiring me to consider the health and wealth of Black America and how we could use the money to change our condition in this country. Last, but surely not least I want to acknowledge Black America. We as a people have come a long way and have even more to go.

Overall I am optimistic about the future of Black America and give endless thanks to my people for the inspiration they bring. Without Black America, I wouldn't have been able to write this book. As a Black American, I was elated to find out all the things we have been and are capable of. It gave me hope for the present and the future in a time I thought we were doomed as a people. Thank you all for your knowledge, wisdom, and insight.

- *A.R Morton*

References

Stanley, Thomas J., and William D. Danko. ***The Millionaire Next Door: The Surprising Secrets of America's Wealthy***. Atlanta, GA: Longstreet, 1996. Print.

Pearson-McNeil, Cheryl, and Saul Rosenberg. ***Increasingly, Affluent, Educated, and Diverse: African-American Consumers: The Untold Story.*** New York City, NY: Nielsen, 2015. Print.

"Cancer Facts & Figures for African Americans." American Cancer Society. American Cancer Society, n.d. Web. 06 Sept. 2016.

"American Time Use Survey Summary." U.S. Bureau of Labor Statistics. U.S. Bureau of Labor Statistics, 24 June 2016. Web. 06 Sept. 2016.

"2016 Restaurant Industry Forecast." National Restaurant Association. National Restaurant Association, n.d. Web. 06 Sept. 2016

Aud, Susan, Fox, Mary Ann, Kewalramani, Angelina. ***"Status and Trends in the Education of Racial and Ethnic Groups."*** US Department of Education. National Center for Education Statistics.

Thompson, Tamika. ***"Fact Sheet: Outcomes for Young, Black Men."*** PBS. PBS, 2014. Web. 06 Sept. 2016.

Toldson, Ivory A., Ph.D., and Chance W. Lewis, Ph.D. ***"Challenge the Status Quo: Academic Success among School-Age African-American Males."*** Washington, DC: *Congressional Black Caucus Foundation*, n.d. Web. 6 Sept. 2016.

Ray, Brian D., Ph.D. ***"Research Facts on Homeschooling."*** *Research Facts on Homeschooling.* National Home Education Research Institute, n.d. Web. 06 Sept. 2016

"How Many People Experience Homelessness?" *National Coalition for the Homeless.* National Coalition for the Homeless, n.d. Web. 07 Sept. 2016.

"Fashion: BLS Spotlight on Statistics." *Fashion: BLS Spotlight on Statistics* (2012) U.S. Bureau of Labor Statistics. U.S. Bureau of Labor Statistics, 2012. Web. 2016.

EJF. (2007). ***"The Deadly Chemicals in Cotton."*** *Environmental Justice Foundation in collaboration with Pesticide Action Network UK*: London, UK. ISBN No. 1-904523-10-2.

Heriot, Gail. ***"Why Aren't There More Black Scientists?"*** *The Wall Street Journal.* Wsj.com, 21 Oct. 2015. Web. 07 Sept. 2016.

Carnevale, Anthony P., Megan L. Fasules, Andrea Porter, and Jennifer Landis-Santos. ***"African Americans College Majors and Earnings."*** (n.d.): n. pag. *Cew.georgetown.edu.* Center on Education and the Workforce, 2016. Web. 2016.

"Digest of Education Statistics." *National Center for Education Statistics.* U.S Department of Education, 2016. Web. 07 Sept. 2016.

"FACT SHEET: Spurring African-American STEM Degree Completion." *U.S Department of Education.* U.S Department of Education, 16 Mar. 2016. Web. 07 Sept. 2016.

"U.S. Entertainment and Media Industry 2011-2020." *Statista.* Statista, 2016. Web. 07 Sept. 2016

"Essential Facts about the Computer and Video Game Industry." *Entertainment Software Association.* Entertainment Software Association, 2015. Web. 2016.

"Xbox One Teardown." *Xbox One Teardown.* TechInsights, Inc., 2016. Web. 08 Sept. 2016.

"Sports, Teams & Leisure Industry Statistics." *Plunkett Research Ltd.* Plunkett Research Ltd, 2016. Web. 08 Sept. 2016.

Badenhausen, Kurt. ***"New York Knicks Head The NBA's Most Valuable Teams At $3 Billion."***

Forbes. Forbes Magazine, 20 Jan. 2016. Web. 08 Sept. 2016.

Cohen, Andrew. ***"How Stadium Construction Costs Reached the Billions."*** *Athletic Business*. Athletic Business Media, Inc., July 2012. Web. 08 Sept. 2016.

Neff, John, and Matthew Dickens. ***"Urban Public Transportation Systems 2013."*** *2013 PUBLIC TRANSPORTATION FACT BOOK (2013)*: 25. *American Public Transportation* Association. American Public Transportation Association, 2013. Web. 08 Sept. 2016.

"Airlines Continue to Improve Profitability 5.1% Net Profit Margin for 2016." *IATA*. International Air Transport Association, 10 Dec. 2015. Web. 08 Sept. 2016.

Weisburd, David, Rosann Greenspan, Edwin Hamilton E., Hubert Williams, and Kellie Bryant A. ***"Police Attitudes toward Abuse of Authority: Findings from a National Study."*** *National Institute of Justice: Research in Brief (2000)*: 3. U.S Department of Justice. U.S Department of Justice, May 2000. Web. Sept. 2016.

"Fires in the U.S." *NFPA Reports.* National Fire Protection Agency, 2016. Web. 08 Sept. 2016.

Orr, Kevyn D. ***Two Year Emergency Manager Budget (2016)***: 1. State of Michigan. City of Detroit, Michigan, 2015. Web. 2016.

Knowles, David. ***"Cost of U.S. Senate Seat: $10.5 Million."*** *NY Daily News*. NY Daily News, 11 Mar. 2013. Web. 08 Sept. 2016.

Kerby, Sophia. ***"The Top 10 Most Startling Facts about People of Color and Criminal Justice in the United States."*** *Center for American Progress.* Center for American Progress, 13 Mar. 2012. Web. 08 Sept. 2016.

Shakur, Ali. ***"Black Businesses: 5 Reasons Why They Fail and Need Celebrities"*** - Hotep: The Meaning and Definition." *Hotep Nation.* Hotep Nation, 21 Sept. 2016. Web. 13 Oct. 2016.

Noel, Reginald A. ***"Income and Spending Patterns among Black Households."*** *U.S. Bureau of Labor Statistics.* U.S.Department of Labor, Nov. 2014. Web. 08 Sept. 2016.

Harish. ***"Meat Consumption Patterns by Race and Gender."*** *Counting Animals*. Counting Animals, 23 Aug. 2012. Web. 08 Sept. 2016.

"Official USDA Food Plans: Cost of Food at Home at Four Levels." *Official USDA Food Plans: Cost of Food at Home at Four Levels, U.S. Average, July 2016* 1 (2016): 1. U.S Department of Agriculture. Center for Nutrition Policy and Promotion, Aug. 2016. Web. 8 Sept. 2016.

Jamrisko, Michelle. ***"Americans' Spending on Dining Out Just Overtook Grocery Sales for the First Time Ever."*** *Bloomberg Markets.* Bloomberg L.P., 14 Apr. 2015. Web. 8 Sept. 2016.

"Experian Marketing Services." *African American Shopper Analysis (2014)*: 4. Experian. Experian

Information Solutions, Inc., 2014. Web. 8 Sept. 2016

Ruetschlin, Catherine, and Dedrick Asante-Muhammad. ***"The Challenge of Credit Card Debt for the African American Middle Class."*** *An Equal Say and an Equal Chance for All.* Demos Org/NAACP, 4 Dec. 2013. Web. 09 Sept. 2016.

Gregoire, Carolyn. ***"Retail Therapy: One In Three Recently Stressed Americans Shops To Deal With Anxiety."*** *The Huffington Post.* TheHuffingtonPost.com, 24 May 2013. Web. 09 Sept. 2016.

"Money Matters on Campus." ***Examining Financial Attitudes and Behaviors of Two-Year and Four-Year College Students*** (n.d.): 9. Money

Matters on Campus. HigherOne / EverFi, 2016. Web. 9 Sept. 2016

Davidson, Kelley. ***"These 7 Household Names Make a Killing Off Prison-Industrial Complex."*** *U.S. Uncut.* U.S Uncut, 30 Aug. 2015. Web. 09 Sept. 2016.

"Federal Bureau of Prisons." *BOP Statistics: Inmate Offenses.* Bureau of Prisons, 25 June 2016. Web. 09 Sept. 2016.

Ellsworth, Scott. ***"Black Wall Street Tulsa's Successful History."*** *Black Wall Street Tulsa History 1830 to 1921.* Black Wall Street Org, n.d. Web. 09 Sept. 2016.

www.ingramcontent.com/pod-product-compliance
Lightning Source LLC
Chambersburg PA
CBHW070312190526
45169CB00005B/1595

* 9 7 8 1 5 3 7 7 9 0 7 8 7 *